GARDEN DIY
WATER FEATURES

MURDOCH
B O O K S

GARDEN DIY
WATER FEATURES

CHRIS MATON
MARK EDWARDS

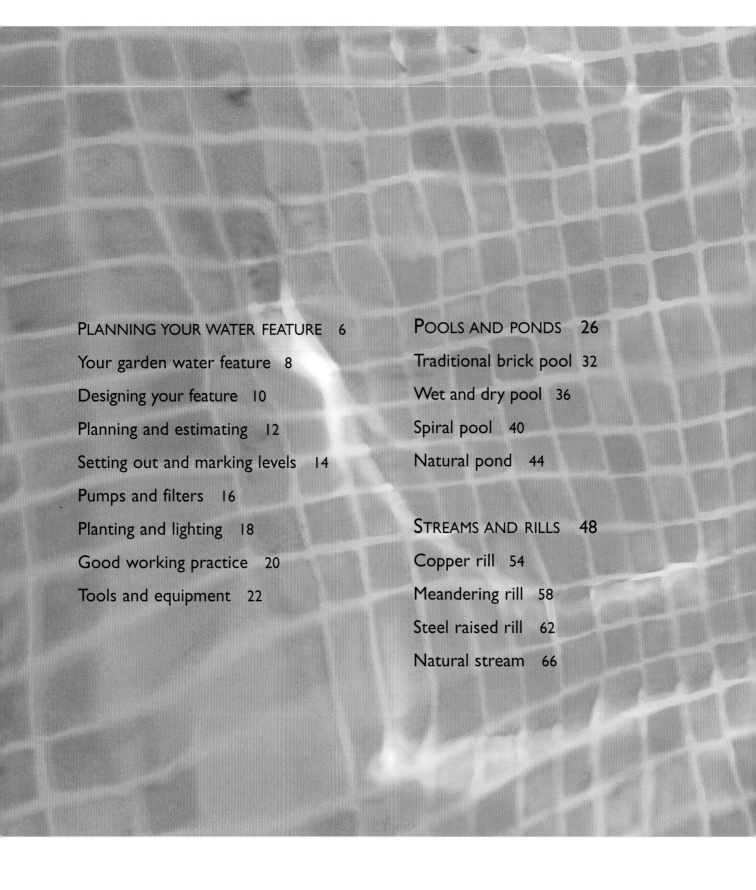

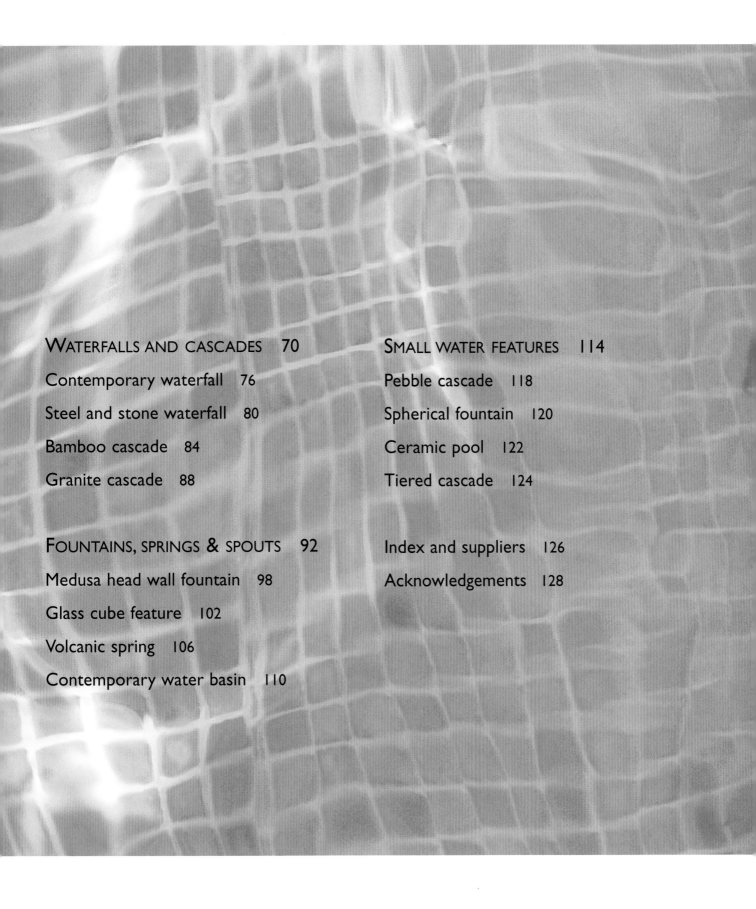

contents

planning your water feature

your garden WATER FEATURE

A well designed water feature is likely to be the focal point of a garden. It therefore gives you the ideal opportunity to create a feature that revitalizes your existing space or, if you are redesigning the whole garden, provides you with a stylish starting point to plan around. The following pages explain how to transform creative ideas into stunning water features.

You can enhance your garden with a beautiful, well designed pond.

Water features are added to gardens for all sorts of reasons. Even if you are very happy with your garden you can use a feature to highlight a particular area or to link two parts of your garden together.

Whatever reason you have for wanting to place a water feature in your garden, there are some simple points to consider that will help you decide which feature is most appropriate for your space. The process of elimination works well here. By looking at the site logically you can easily come up with a few suitable choices.

This book takes you through all the stages of planning, design and construction – removing the pitfalls commonly associated with the selection and practical inclusion of water in the garden.

Using this book

The information and projects covered in this book will inspire and challenge the conventional ideas surrounding water feature design and construction. Although natural features are included here, the majority of our gardens are just too small to incorporate this style with any conviction. This book therefore uses more realistic features that can be included in all our modern-day gardens.

The first section covers the basic information that you will need to plan and complete your project, from how to find the style that most suits you and your specific site through to practical knowledge of how to ensure that your feature is safe for children.

Correct construction is as essential as a suitable design as it will prevent unnecessary water leaks and allow the project to last the test of time. All of the know-how you will need to do this is given. There is no such thing as a maintenance-free water feature and so this section also covers ways that you can keep your new feature looking good and working well throughout the seasons.

The main section of the book looks at 20 practical and inspirational features that represent distinct styles of construction for all the various types of gardens. Diverse subjects include fountains, springs and spouts, waterfalls and mini-projects for smaller gardens. The construction of these designs is clearly explained using step-by-step photography. Incorporated into these sections are practical techniques as well as some alternative material suggestions that may suit your style or preferences more closely. These should also inspire you to use your own creativity to tailor the basic project ideas to your own specific space.

Before you begin

Even before you start the practical part of the project, you will need to establish the type of skills you require to complete the feature. Water features are different to many other garden features as almost all of them require more than one practical ability. This does not mean that you shouldn't tackle a water feature yourself but you should look realistically at your repertoire. If you are in any doubt about the tasks ahead, contact your local tradespeople as they will be able to help with the parts that you feel less confident about. Always ensure that you get several quotes and build these into the overall project budget.

Take a look at the area around the site that you plan to build on, as there may be other areas that you need to plant and pave in order to create the cohesive design you are after. Occasionally, you may need an extra pair of hands to lift heavy objects and make life more bearable – bear this in mind when you plan the project.

Budgetary requirements

It is surprising how the cost of garden projects can accumulate. Water features predominantly involve hard landscaping, which is the most expensive part of any garden both in terms of labour and materials. However, careful planning can prevent any nasty shocks. Materials and tool hire will absorb most of your budget and, if you need to bring in specialist labour, such as an electrician, you must make allowances for this.

It is vital to plan methodically, making lists of materials, labour requirements and any possible tool hire you may need. Then you can adjust costs where necessary. For example, look at the materials you have chosen to use as there may be cheaper options available, such as reproduction stone instead of natural, or replace second-hand bricks with modern imitations. If you are installing a small feature, solar pumps will eliminate the need for an electrician and an excavated, lined pool with cleverly planted edges will be far more cost effective than one constructed from rendered blocks.

Materials should be chosen to reflect your budget.

Finding unusual materials

Inspiration for water features is all around you. Take a look at books or magazines and visit garden shows to give you ideas. Specialist aquatic centres, for example, sell an ever-expanding range of products, but avoid the temptation to impulse buy as this often results in taking products home that will not actually suit the garden. There is a huge range of water features and associated materials available on the Internet too and these are generally cheaper because the site does not have any shop overheads to pay.

You can stumble across amazing one-off items for reservoirs or water chutes by visiting your local reclamation yard. By combining these older artifacts with much more contemporary materials, such as glass tiles, you can create a personalized water feature that suits your taste and garden specifically. Scrap metal yards are also useful places to look if you want to experiment with abstract materials. It may be a weird-looking spout that just lifts and makes your feature spring to life…

Tiles can be used to great effect in water features.

designing YOUR FEATURE

Exciting and dynamic, water dramatically changes the mood and atmosphere of a garden so you should take your time when choosing the style and position of your feature. Consider its shape, size and finished level and try to keep it simple – over-complicated designs tend to be at odds with a garden while a simple design blends in much more easily.

Style

The style of water feature you choose will depend on you – your likes and dislikes, passions and personal experiences relating to water. You may remember a beautiful rambling brook from a country visit or a stunning formal pool seen on a recent holiday. There are many ways to take these images and personalize the ideas behind them to create your own feature. Be bold and express yourself.

In general, the style of water features falls into two main categories: formal and informal. Perhaps the easier to achieve, formal features link more convincingly with the house and surrounding manmade features of a garden. This gives you opportunities to experiment with abstract materials

An informal pond in a natural setting.

and ideas, to create a strong architectural presence. Informal designs are better suited further away from the building, where planting and nature can interact without the dominance of the house.

Position

If you are redesigning your whole garden it is important to tackle the question of where to place the water feature early on. If you have an area in the garden that just needs lifting, some important questions need to be answered before you begin. The following factors are the kinds of things to consider when choosing the final position.

Trees and buildings

Are there large trees in your garden (or a neighbour's garden) that may shade your water feature during the day or have roots that could damage the foundations of your feature? Fallen leaves and poisonous berries will pollute the water and poison fish, so think about the species of plants that exist around the area and those you may want to introduce.

Most pools and ponds will need a minimum of half a day's sunlight for oxygenating plants to perform their job. If this is unlikely given the position, filters can be used (see pages 16–17).

Town gardens also suffer from tall neighbouring buildings, which cast heavy shade over much of the garden, but fountains and moving water will help the oxygenating process in such

Moving water will help the oxygenating process.

a situation. Take a note of the shade position every couple of hours during a whole day by marking the shadows with canes and then do a rough sketch of the garden to find potential sites based on the results.

Views

Positioning your feature to get the best views from the house and within the garden will make the most of what's on offer. Think about which room you view the garden from most or decide if you want to screen the feature from the house for a sense of mystery when you are in the garden.

If you would like to see the reflection of a tree or building on the water's surface from a particular viewing position then try laying a mirror on the ground in order to locate the reflection. It helps to position some canes or pots in the potential area and then to leave them in place for a few days. See how you feel about where the reflection appears and adjust or move the intended site if you are not entirely happy. Remember that once the feature has been constructed there is no going back so take your time when choosing the site.

Existing site

Make a note of manholes, services and outside taps. If you are in any doubt about locating these, contact your service supplier for engineers to confirm the positions. They will also locate any cables and pipes that may interfere with excavations.

If you have a windy site it can make sitting in the area uncomfortable and also completely ruin delicate spray patterns and filmy waterfalls. If you have to place your feature in such a site then think about filtering the wind with planting or a creative screen or backdrop.

Decide which existing features you wish to keep as you may find that your preferred water feature fights with some of them. This applies particularly to upright designs, which are very contemporary. If you place one right next to a traditional pergola it will look at odds with it.

Compacted and rocky soil will make serious work of any large-scale excavations needed for pools and

ponds so if your site is full of it then a wall fountain may be more appropriate. You should dig a 600mm (2ft) deep test hole to look at the natural water table. If the level is high, it may cause flexible liners to billow up. This can be overcome by placing heavy slabs on the area, but it is better to relocate the feature or choose another style as trying to control ground water levels can be costly and time-consuming.

To help you when you come to choose plants to complement the feature, make a note of the pH levels in the surrounding soil.

Think about the shortest route for electricity supply from the house, garage or shed – do you need to chisel out huge amounts of concrete to get to the feature? It is often best to consult a qualified electrician for advice on such electrical matters.

Material choice

It cannot be emphasized enough how much your choice of materials will influence the look of your feature. When deciding on what to use look at the durability of the product and how it ages – natural stone, for example, wears more sympathetically than concrete. The cost will of course be an important influence on your final choice but try to buy at the top end of your budget as your feature will then look more professional and stand the test of time.

Also look to your site to give you ideas – materials such as brick walls and flagstones already in the garden will work well in your feature too. You can also look beyond your own garden boundaries to materials from the local environment or traditional industries such as steel or pottery.

Safety

Water seems to have a magnetic quality for children so safety is extremely important. There are some points to remember if the two are definitely going to meet.

Choose features that can be covered with a grid and cobbles such as wall fountains, springs and cascades. If you decide to construct a raised pool then build the walls at least 600mm (2ft) high and overhang coping stones. If you really want an open water feature, make sure that the garden you create has a separated area with childproof locks or catches.

A raised pool with a tiled, overhung edge.

As an extra precaution use a grid just under the water's surface, strong enough to support a child's weight.

Make pool edges as safe as possible by using heavy marginal planting to create a physical barrier. A shallow, gravel-edged feature is safe because of the gentle gradients to the edge.

Natural stone is prone to slime up, whereas concrete flags have a much better grip so are more appropriate. You should also check that edging stones or copings are well laid and mortared to prevent tipping.

planning AND ESTIMATING

Carefully planning your water feature will ensure that you don't have any nasty surprises during its construction. Now that the design and style of your feature has been chosen, you will need to break the project down and think seriously about all the practical implications that range from ordering a specialist component through to dealing with poor weather.

Estimating time

It is sensible to double the amount of time you think you will need for the planning and constructing of your water feature as this gives a more realistic time period. Remember you must add all the ordering, visits to suppliers and general phone calls to your estimate.

You should also make allowances for unforeseen events such as machinery breakdowns or the odd downpour that floods your garden. There will be other factors beyond your control, such as how booked up a tradesperson is if you need specialist labour. Also bear in mind that it takes time to set things up in the morning and tidy the site at the end of each day.

If you allow yourself extra time in the planning stages then you can relax and enjoy the job. This should also ensure that you finish on time (or even early), instead of rushing around getting worked up and frustrated.

Estimating tools and materials

Establishing the quantities of materials you need early on will give you a good idea of how much your feature will cost. Do this at the planning stage to avoid wasting time and money.

Make a thorough list of the materials needed and find out when your chosen supplier can deliver. Delivery times range from a couple of days after ordering for general cement and sand, and up to four to six weeks for more specialist items that need to be made to your specifications. Suppliers are generally willing to help quantify materials. If you give them a sketch and some rough sizes they should be able to help you.

Concrete

Concrete is usually measured as a volume so, in order to calculate how much you want, you need to know what the area of the base is and then multiply that by the depth of concrete. Unless you are ordering a huge amount you can probably mix your own 20mm (³⁄₄in) ballast, cement and water together to form concrete. Mix a ratio of 1:6 (one part cement to six parts ballast) in a mixer or by hand.

Order the total foundation quantity in ballast then order 10 bags of cement per cubic metre (12 per cubic yard) – there is no extra volume of concrete as the cement particles fill any voids in the aggregate. Store the ballast on a hard surface and cover it with sheeting. Cement can be placed on a pallet in a shed or garage.

Bricks and blocks

These materials are measured by calculating the number needed per square metre (or yard) so establish the area of the wall you wish to build and multiply by the number of bricks or blocks per square metre. For example, for a half brick thick wall you will need 60 bricks per sq m (50 bricks per sq yard). For a concrete block wall you will need 10 blocks per sq m (12 blocks per sq yard).

Bricks and blocks should always be safely stacked on pallets then covered with plastic until they are used.

Mortars

Used for rendering or brick- and block laying, mortars are made up of cement, building or pit sand and water. An additive is often also used to help with the workability of the mortar.

Store pit sand on a flat surface, separated from stony ballast, as it can be annoying to keep fishing out stones from your rendering or

Mortar mixes

The following mixes are recommended.

Brick- and block laying below ground: 1 part cement to 3 or 4 parts sand

Brick- and block laying above ground: 1 part cement to 6 parts sand

Rendering walls: 1 part cement to 6 parts sand

Rendering pools: 1 part cement to 4 parts sand (with added fibre reinforcement)

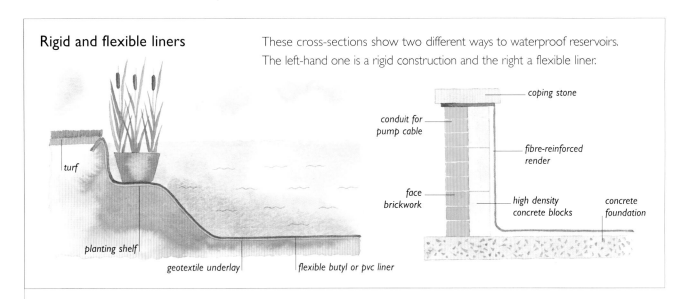

Rigid and flexible liners

These cross-sections show two different ways to waterproof reservoirs. The left-hand one is a rigid construction and the right a flexible liner.

turf

planting shelf

geotextile underlay

flexible butyl or pvc liner

coping stone

conduit for pump cable

fibre-reinforced render

face brickwork

high density concrete blocks

concrete foundation

---

bricklaying mix. Some sand can stain driveways so a plastic sheet underneath is advisable.

Pointing

This is the process of filling the joints in paving and brickwork to achieve a weatherproof, attractive appearance. Brick joints are pointed with a mix of one part cement to four or five parts building or soft washed sand, whereas paving mortar is slightly stronger. This has a ratio of 1:3 and is a dryish mix, used to avoid staining the slabs.

Timber

Where at all possible, order pressure-treated timber for any exterior use – this may not be possible when you are using planed or one-off sizes so any non-pressure-treated pieces will need treating with clear or coloured preservative at some stage. Ordered by the linear metre (foot), you should store your timber on a flat surface in a dry or covered storage area.

Specialist products

Some of the water features in this book have components that need to be ordered from more unusual suppliers like stone merchants. These need ordering weeks in advance. Also, remember to take into account that one-off items from reclamation yards may need cleaning before being used.

Reservoirs

Every water feature has a reservoir of some description that the main body of water is held in and pumped from. There are many ways to create one but here are two basic techniques.

Rigid construction

Used for many formal pools, the strength and durability of this style of construction gives you a number of alternatives as it can be incorporated into raised pools, multiple cascades or a simple ground level reflective pool. The cost of construction is high because you may need specialist labour and building materials, but the diversity often outweighs this cost.

Flexible lined pools and ponds

Flexible liners are mainly used in naturalized ponds. They obviously cost much less than the rigid constructions

do because there is no need for concrete, bricks and mortar.

Liners are available in different grades but it is worth spending as much as you can afford on a quality one as this will save you from costly repair bills later on. Less expensive materials tend to degrade and become brittle due to UV rays present in sunlight. Ask your local supplier's advice and ensure the item you buy has a 10–15 year guarantee.

Calculating liners and fleece

The size of the liner that you will need can be calculated by adding twice the depth of the pool to the length and to the width. You should then add a tolerance of 300mm (1ft) to these figures.

So, for a pool measuring 3.6 x 2.2m (12 x 7½ft) and 700mm (2⅓ft) deep, the calculation would be:

700mm (2½ft) x 2 = 1.4m (4⅔ft)
+ Length of 3.6m (12ft)
+ Tolerance of 300mm (1ft)
= 5.3m (17¾ft) length

700mm (2½ft) x 2 = 1.4m (4⅔ft)
+ Width of 2.2m (7½ft)
+ Tolerance of 300mm (1ft)
= 3.9m (13ft) width

setting out AND MARKING LEVELS

Once you have picked your water feature and have quantified and estimated the project, you are ready to start the physical work. Some initial clearance of debris and overgrown foliage may be required to help you see the entire area, to establish surrounding levels and to set out the outline for your excavations, which is a vital part of the process.

Using the 3,4,5 method

There is a quick and easy method to create a perfect rectangle or square. Once you know it, you can mark out anything from a set of coping stones above a sunken pool right through to a football pitch – it is the same method, the 3, 4, 5 method.

1 You can carry out 90 percent of all your setting out by creating a 90° right angle. Start by making a base line that is 1m (3ft) longer than the proposed excavation, which can then be referred to at any time. You can eventually use this line for the front of your water feature, so check it is facing the right way and that you are happy with the position. Fix in a peg at each end of the line and pull the line tight between them.

2 The width of the excavation can be marked on the base line by driving in two extra pegs. Make up a large timber square with the length of the sides being multiples of 3, 4 and 5. Usually a square measuring 900, 1200 and 1500mm (3, 4 and 5ft) is adequate. The square should be placed on the base line at your excavation peg to give you your 90° offset. Now mark the excavation length along this line using string and a peg.

3 Repeat this process beside the other peg on the base line in order to form a parallel string line. You can then finish off the rectangle by fixing a taut line to the remaining side. Next, make sure that you check each side is correctly measured and that the diagonals are equal.

4 Spread a line of sand beneath the string lines so that you can remove all string before excavating. It is useful to extend the string outside the area so that you can bang in reference pegs. Afterwards, the string lines can be used to set out other heights or lengths.

Marking out a circle

You may need to mark out circles or segments of circles when setting out the feature. It is quite straightforward – just locate your centre point first.

1 Unless you have a scaled plan with your feature plotted on the paper, you will need to establish where the pool is going on your site. Insert a cane in the centre of the proposed pool and slip a tape over the end of the cane to keep it in place. Check that the radius will fit the plot. Adjust if needed.

2 Tie a screwdriver to the tape. Then scribe the surface, laying a sand line or spray for extra definition as necessary.

Irregular shapes

If you are constructing a wildlife or naturalistic pond, organic and free-flowing shapes will blend in better than hard geometric lines do. These shapes are sometimes difficult to get right so it pays to take some time to achieve the best looking form for your site.

Once your area is cleared of all debris and obstructions, lay a hose or some canes placed at 1m (3ft) centres around the perimeter of your pond. Don't worry about getting it absolutely perfect at the moment. Have a walk around and see if the shape works for your plot and check that there is enough room around the margins for planting and maintenance tasks. To do this, try and get a bird's eye view of the pond from either inside the house or up a ladder. This will also give you a better idea of the scale and position of the feature within its location. It will show up any tight curves that are difficult to build and anything that looks at odds in a natural environment too. As a rule, try to keep curves soft and long.

Make any adjustments to the pond and doublecheck the shape – you can now lay a thin line of sand to join up the canes or replace the hose line.

Site clearance

Your project will undoubtedly involve a certain amount of clearance as existing rubble and vegetation will need to be removed from the site. If you plan to install a pool or feature in an existing patio, make sure that you carefully cut the stone work with a diamond-tipped slab cutter.

A large natural pond may need an excavator, so you should check the site for access as you may need to board out some areas of the garden in order to protect the soil when you bring it in. Even if you do not have machinery on site, a lot of serious damage can be caused to the soil structure and surrounding areas by feet compaction, especially in wet weather conditions. Therefore avoid digging in these particular conditions. Valuable topsoil should be stored for use at a later date once it is stripped.

Levels

The height of a water feature generally relates to its surrounding ground level. Therefore, once the feature has been set out, a datum or reference peg can be installed 500–1000mm (1³/₄–3ft) away from any excavations.

Using a lump hammer, knock the peg into the ground making sure it is upright and stable. The length of the peg will depend on the height of the feature. Once the peg is in position you will need to mark off against the peg the height of foundations, final paving or gravel finishes.

As you build your construction make sure you check against the datum peg in order to ensure the accuracy of your work.

Place a datum peg next to your excavations.

pumps AND FILTERS

You will find a vast selection of pumps, filters and associated fittings for every imaginable type of water feature at any aquatic centre. Rather than spend hours thumbing through the sometimes mind-boggling product information, you should visit your supplier armed with specific information regarding your water feature.

Buying equipment

Choosing the right pumps and filters can be quite daunting and costly if you have never done it before. So once you have decided on your feature, make a sketch of what you want and write down various facts about the feature. Then talk to your local aquarist and they will advise on technical issues such as pump capacity and type. In order to help the supplier find you the right pump and fittings it is a good idea to ask yourself the following questions before you go: what is the size of your pool or feature (i.e. the volume of water to be circulated)? What height do you want your water jet (fountain) to be? What is the difference in height between the pump and the outlet (head of water)? Will the pump be working continuously or intermittently?

Introducing pumps

There are two types of pumps available, submersible and surface pumps. The efficiency and cheap running costs of submersibles means that 99 percent of all water features use this type. Surface-mounted pumps are mainly used in swimming pool construction, major commercial water features and in situations where large volumes need to be circulated. They can be noisy and need to be placed in a dry, ventilated, purpose-made housing, which creates more work, expense and complicated pipework.

It is a good idea to buy a pump that has a flow adjuster built into it. Alternatively, you can connect a flow valve on an outlet hose close to the pump. This adjustable pump gives you the option of fine tuning the amount of water that is being moved, which is especially useful for wall features and fountains.

Filters

In natural and many minimalist designs the key to achieving a successful feature is the clarity of the water. One of the main causes of frustration with still water is its tendency to cloud over and stagnate. Bacteria, algae and waste products do build up quickly and affect water quality.

There are many chemical products that clear the water for a few weeks, but the water will need re-dosing, which becomes expensive in the long term and is not a particularly pleasant task. Although seen as an unnecessary initial expense, a filter is therefore often more appropriate. Filtration can also be used to aid the natural oxygenating quality of plants, especially in the first couple of years when a pond is establishing its own in-built eco-system.

A filter works by slowly recycling the body of water. This can be carried out intermittently or continuously depending on the size and type of feature. The pump simply pumps

A submersible pump for recirculating water.

A bio-media filtration unit removes algae.

water within the pool to the top of a filter unit. The water then passes through fine layers of bio-media, which purify the water and then returns to the pool via an outlet at the base of the unit. Gravity is used to return the water so the filter will need to be placed at a minimum of 500mm (1³/₄ft) above the pool. Filtration units are not very attractive, so think about screening yours with plants or some other form of trellis or fencing.

If additional clarity is needed, for example in a reflection pool or Koi pond, the use of a UV clarifier is recommended. This can be attached to the side of the filter, the water then passes into the UV unit where ultraviolet radiation makes algae clump together so it can be strained out by the filter.

Electricity

Unless you are using a solar pump, which are really only suitable for small features because of their low output, you will need to install electricity at some stage. This is a great opportunity to install a ring main (a power cable that travels around the whole of the garden), particularly if you are designing your garden from scratch. Not only does it make it easier to plan the route and dig trenches, it gives you the scope to introduce lighting and so add another dimension to the garden. Any cable in the ground should either be armoured or laid in conduit and be placed at least 600mm (2ft) down so that it is out of the reach of forks and spades. Cables laid under paving need ducting for protection and to allow you to replace them should you need to in the future.

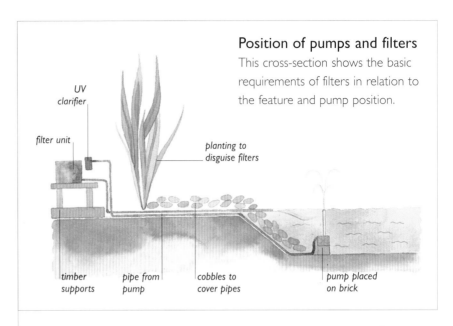

Position of pumps and filters
This cross-section shows the basic requirements of filters in relation to the feature and pump position.

UV clarifier

filter unit

planting to disguise filters

timber supports

pipe from pump

cobbles to cover pipes

pump placed on brick

If you are placing the water feature close to the house, you can run the electrical feed from the nearest socket indoors. If you do this, you will need a circuit breaker before it leaves the house in order to meet legal and safety requirements. Low voltage pumps are available for small features and fountains but you will need a transformer to reduce the power and make them safe for use outdoors. This should be placed next to the socket.

It is essential that all connections are carried out professionally because of the safety implications. Therefore it is usually best to employ a qualified electrician for this part of the project.

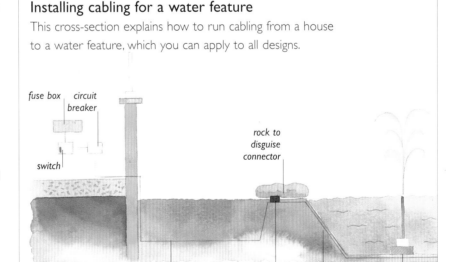

Installing cabling for a water feature
This cross-section explains how to run cabling from a house to a water feature, which you can apply to all designs.

fuse box

circuit breaker

rock to disguise connector

switch

armoured cable

weatherproof connector

pump cable

pump placed on brick

planting and LIGHTING

Planting can make all the difference to your project, by enhancing it and creating connections to other parts of the garden. Water features also lend themselves beautifully to the subtle and sometimes magical effects that you can create with the right lighting. Both the features themselves and surrounding plants can be transformed into dramatic shapes at night.

Planting around water features

The water feature will be the focus of attention within the garden, so neighbouring plants should complement and enhance rather than confuse and dominate. A good rule of thumb is to keep things simple. When planting around any water feature use bold clumps and fewer species. This works far better than a confusing mixed bag of many varieties. Try to use a higher proportion of evergreen plants such as *Prunus lusitanica*, which will create a stable framework around the feature, especially during winter.

In small gardens, where the water feature is positioned close to the boundary, allow an area for planting directly behind it. This will create a backdrop that will hold your view of the water. And partially screening the front of water features with slender strap-like plants can create a feeling of mystery.

Planting in water

The balance and clarity of a natural pond relies greatly on a diverse range of plants. Plant categories for ponds are arranged by the conditions each type prefers.

Deep-water aquatics such as lilies can be planted in aquatic baskets in deep, central parts of the pool. They have their roots at the bottom of the pool and their leaves float on the surface. They are ideal for reducing algae growth in the pond as they cut down the sunlight that algae needs to thrive. Aim to cover around half of the water's surface with such plants.

Waterlilies are deep-water aquatic plants.

Submerged plants such as *Callitriche autumnalis* are also planted in deep areas and are most important for oxygenating and preventing water stagnation. They compete with algae for sunlight and nutrients and also helpfully exchange carbon dioxide for oxygen.

Marginal plants such as *Glyceria maxima* are planted on shelves within aquatic baskets where their roots should stay constantly wet and their foliage should be above the water line.

Planting styles

Your feature will dictate the style of planting you choose. Formal pools and fountains benefit from clipped evergreen planting, perhaps in the form of a surrounding hedge or topiary strategically placed to balance the geometry. If you are creating a minimalist contemporary pool, use a single specimen or stick to a single species on mass to keep the style clean. Informal designs lend themselves to more herbaceous planting.

Reflections

Plants form intriguing compositions when mirrored on water. Single specimen planting looks dramatic if reflected on still clear pools. Grasses look really at home when planted in drifts around the edge.

The sun's reflection can actually create hostile conditions for plants as it kicks back sunlight onto the underside of delicate leaves, causing them to scorch and lose excessive amounts of water. If your feature is in a sunny spot, include grey- and silver-leafed planting as this can naturally cope with such hostile environments.

Lighting techniques

Subtlety is everything in lighting – the football stadium technique, while great at stopping intruders, can be a bit much for the average garden. Whether you choose a single, well directed beam or dozens of randomly placed candles and tea lights, the result will be far more satisfying.

Pools and ponds

Still dark water has the ability to duplicate any surrounding planting and even the size of background walls and architecture are amplified. The key here is to uplight the subject using discretely positioned spotlights, keeping the angle of the beam low. This casts long shadows that provide depth and texture, as well as enhancing a plant's architectural structure. You can also place the light source directly behind a plant to silhouette it across the water's surface. Shining light straight onto still water, however, causes glare; it is better to downlight the pool.

When placing lighting under water remember that everything will be illuminated – including rocks, plants and pumps. If your water lacks clarity, your pool may resemble primeval soup. Underwater fittings can also become grimy, which reduces their effectiveness, so they do need regular

Lighting by water can be extremely effective.

cleaning. Position them on the perimeter facing the centre to make sure they are accessible for cleaning.

Fountains, springs and moving water

Jets and fountains can be lit in several ways. An upward-angled spotlight from the side catches the movement of water beautifully. Place the fitting within adjacent borders or behind strategically placed pots, as the idea is to see the effect rather than the fitting.

If you are after sheer drama, luminous effects are achieved by placing lamps below fountains and behind waterfalls. The use of a tight beam shining upwards, placed just under the surface, creates the illusion of light clinging to the water. When using this technique, it helps to keep the background as dark as possible.

Practical considerations

When using lighting in and around a water feature there are many practical points that need addressing.

Cables and switches

Most lighting schemes can be run off the cable used for the pump. It is always best to install four-cored cabling as the pump and lighting can then be used completely independently, which is important if the lighting is to be tackled later on. It is a good idea to position switches inside the house as this is much more convenient in the winter, for example, when you want to see the feature lit in the evenings.

As with all external wiring, circuit breakers are needed and any cables in the ground need to be armoured and placed in a trench at least 600mm (2ft) below ground level. You should get a qualified electrician to do this.

What type of lighting?

Manufacturers have realized the huge market in outdoor lighting due to the increasing desire of people to use their garden at nighttime. They now produce an ever-increasing range.

Low voltage Operating through a transformer, these lights are excellent if you have a paved courtyard and need an alternative to chiselling out miles of thick concrete. However, if the lights are positioned too far away from the transformer, the voltage drop results in reduced performance, which means they best suit smaller gardens.

Mains If you want to have larger lighting schemes, or wish to view your feature from a distance, then use your mains supply to give you greater illuminating power. The extra capacity allows you to uplight trees and use multiple lights to create subtle effects.

Fibre-optics These lights also run off the mains. The light source comes from a bright projector lamp inside a box, which should be positioned discretely outside the water feature. The light then travels along flexible single or multiple fibre-optic rods. Because the rods are flexible, you can bend and position the light source.

Products

Try to choose fittings that are dark and have a matt finish as these are easier to conceal and often less expensive. If there is no way of hiding the fitting, it best to use high-quality units made from brass, copper or brushed stainless steel.

Coloured lamps and bulbs, while initially attention grabbing, soon become tiresome. Plants and water absorb and reflect white light much better (depending on the surface), giving clean, simple, professional results.

good WORKING PRACTICE

The smooth running of a project involves very careful planning so that you have everything where you need it before you begin. It will also ensure that you and your family are safe while you construct your exciting project. And, once built, you will need to keep your water feature looking its best through regular maintenance.

Safety

Speak to anyone working in the landscaping industry and you will hear tales of chronic back problems and minor injuries. These are, of course, not intentional, but there are many ways you can prevent them from happening to you.

Before you start work, do a quick risk assessment of the day's work to open your eyes to potential hazards. Think about who is at risk, what jobs you are going to carry out and the tools that will be used. Finally assess how you can minimize any risks.

Poor lifting technique causes most back injuries. So when you are lifting a heavy object crouch down, lift using your legs and keep your back straight. Try to keep the object as close to

Make sure you lift heavy objects properly.

your body as possible and avoid lifting and twisting your back. Have a slow stretch before you start work and avoid jobs that involve lifting huge weights straight away – warm up first.

Make sure that you have protective clothing – steel toe-capped boots, overalls and strong gloves will be useful in most construction projects. Tie back long hair and always use goggles, ear defenders and breathing masks when cutting stone and metal.

When using any electrical equipment use a circuit breaker for your and your property's protection. Unless solar powered, most water features will have electrical requirements at some stage, so get advice from, or use, a qualified electrician at all times.

It is likely that your project will be the centre of attention in the garden while it is being constructed, especially if you have children, so keep an eye on all sharp tools and electrical equipment and lock them away at night. As you will have excavations and holes to start with, make sure that they are covered with strong boards each night and cordon off the area.

Materials

You should try to store materials as near as you can to where you will use them. Also avoid handling materials

more than once as this takes time and increases the chances of damage. Always stack bricks, blocks and timber safely on flat areas and preferably cover them with plastic as they will then be clean and easy to use.

Ensure that materials are stacked on flat areas.

It is unlikely that you will need huge amounts of sand and aggregate so order them in 40kg (88lb) bags and try to store them off the ground. If you are using loose deliveries, tip them onto some ply sheeting or a hard-standing area, but cover the area with plastic first as some sands stain. Segregate different sands to keep the correct consistency when mixing mortars and concrete. Cement should be stored off the ground and covered with plastic, ideally in a shed or garage.

Working on site

Planning will make your day's work more productive and enjoyable. Try to build up a realistic work programme before you start, taking into account labour, material and tool requirements.

Remember that noise travels a long way outside and neighbours might not appreciate you drilling and hammering early on a Sunday morning. Plan noisy stages and jobs for later in the day.

As the work proceeds, stop for regular five minute sessions to have a tidy up. This will ensure you keep hazards out of the way. At the end of the day, have a good clean up. Make sure that you clean mixers and spades so that they are free of concrete, protect excavations and cover mortars and cements that might be damaged by rain or frosts.

Maintenance and repair

Once you have completed your water feature you need to keep it looking its best throughout the seasons.

Still water

The biggest problem with still water is the continual build up of algae, which thrives on sunlight and mineral salts

Make sure you remove any excess algae.

within the water. Cloudiness and green water can be removed in different ways. In planted pools and ponds, use oxygenating aquatics and floating lilies to provide shade (see page 18). Where plants interfere with the style of a reflective pool, filters and UV clarifiers can be used. Proprietary solutions and algaecides are effective when added to smaller pools, but will need re-dosing at regular intervals.

Moving water

Fountains, waterfalls and moving water provide less opportunity for algae growth, as the water is agitated and the water reservoir often cut off from direct sunlight. However, you will still need to clean out the reservoirs of all debris and deleterious material occasionally. You should also replace the water, which can smell if left.

Other considerations

In winter ice will cause damage to wildlife and pool structures, preventing the exchange of oxygen in the water and creating considerable pressure on the sides of walls. To combat this, place a couple of black plastic balls on the water's surface. These will absorb any heat emitted from the sun, melt the surrounding ice and also take up the expanding ice sheet.

Moving water is less likely to ice up but it still may be best to turn the feature off over the few coldest months. If you do, remove, clean and dry the pump to prevent damage.

Pumps, filters and lights

By regularly checking your pump cables, electrical connections and filters for damage or blockages, you will reduce costly replacements to a minimum. Light fittings and lenses

Remove and clean the pump regularly.

require cleaning once in a while, so wipe off any algae and slime attracted by the heat of the fitting.

Surrounding materials

The surroundings also have their own maintenance requirements. For example, timber may need re-staining or treating and metalwork may develop rust spots and flaky patches. Stainless steel could need baby oil applied to it to remove smudges or a wipe over with window cleaner.

After inspecting brickwork, the occasional joint may need re-pointing. If so, take care to match the joint colour. Stone flags around pool edges may become loose so test them for stability and re-lay as necessary.

Tool maintenance

Spades, chisels and hammers that are well looked after will give you years of reliable use. Check the handles and shafts for splits and stability and lightly oil all metal surfaces before storing them in a dry place over winter. Also inspect cables and working parts regularly on electrical equipment and remember to take them to a tool hire shop annually for a service.

tools and EQUIPMENT

Always try to buy quality tools, as these will last a lifetime. The following tool lists are broken down into the three main sections that are mentioned in the projects: groundwork, building and wood-/metalwork. There are also details of power tools that you may buy or hire. The tools featured in the photographs are described directly above the images.

Groundwork tools

Bow saw This large toothed saw is for cutting out large unwanted shrubs and small to medium trees.

Crow bar This tool is ideal for levering concrete and brickwork out.

First aid kit Before the start of any building work, this kit needs to be checked and then kept at hand in case of emergencies. It is useful to include emergency telephone numbers within the kit and make sure you are familiar with the general principles and procedures of first aid.

Fork A sturdy heavy-duty fork is used for breaking out hard ground. A planting fork would not be sufficient for groundwork.

Garden rake The rake is essential for moving and levelling beds as well as removing unwanted debris.

Hand loppers Loppers are used to cut the limbs of trees and shrubs that are too big for garden snips. Sharpen and oil the blades and joints regularly.

Hand rammer This tool is used for compacting small areas of hardcore and road.

Mattock This looks similar to a pick axe. One of the sides has a spade-like head and is best used for digging out channels and trench work. The other is like the head of an axe and is great for removing unwanted roots.

Pick axe This tool is used for cracking through and breaking out old concrete and very hard ground.

Sledgehammer This has a large solid steel head attached to a long shaft handle, which is used for driving in and smashing up materials.
Spade This is the best tool for edging work in trenches and hole digging.
Tape measures The hand tape is essential for all construction measurements as well as triangulation

work. Large reel tapes are used for setting out and pinpointing reference points in the garden.
Treated timber pegs These short lengths of timber, which are normally 450mm (1½ft), are used for installing levels, marking and setting out.

Wheel barrow and shovel The wheel barrow is needed for carrying heavy loads. You should buy one with an inflated tyre as this will cope with the weight more easily. The shovel, with its large plate and sides, is ideal for loading loose material and is also helpful for spreading hardcore and mortar.

Building tools
Bolt croppers These are used to cut through reinforced road mesh and road pins.
Bricklaying trowel This is used to lay and spread mortar.

Builders' square A wooden triangular frame used to set out corners.
Club hammer and chisels The club hammer has many uses such as breaking bricks and driving pegs in. The handle can also be used for tamping down paving stones. Chisels are used for cutting and chopping out various stone or brick surfaces. Use them for removing concrete channels when installing ducting.

Craft knife This is used for cutting butyl liners and protective fleece.

Levels You should ideally purchase two of these – a 1m (3ft) level and a smaller boat level for handy use.

Lines and pins Pins refer to the short metal pins onto which a string line can be attached at both ends. This is then used to show level, height and direction by being pushed into soil, mortar joints in brickwork or at the ends of paving.

Plasterer's hawk and float The hawk is used to hold mortar next to the surface it is being applied to. The float is a levelling and smoothing tool used to apply mortar to walls.

Plastic sheets Sheets are used to cover up work in bad weather and will also protect it from on-site debris.

Pointing trowel and tool This trowel is for pointing paving and brickwork. The pointing tool is half rounded like a hose – this is rubbed over mortar to give a particular finish.

Safety equipment This gear is a must and includes a breathing mask, eye protectors and ear guards. Make sure that you wear them whenever you are instructed or advised to. For example, you should always ensure that you protect your ears and eyes when cutting through materials such as stone.

Straightedge A straightedge can be made from hardwood or, more often, steel. It is used on its own to quickly check for consistent level or can be used alongside a level for more accurate results.

Tool belt This is very useful for carrying fixings, fittings and hand tools around as it frees up your hands.

Wood- and metalwork tools

Claw hammer A claw hammer is used to drive in and remove nails.

Hacksaw This saw is used for cutting copper and other metals, which is particularly useful when you are dealing with pipework.

Hand clamp Used to keep materials together when drilling or cutting – it is basically a second 'pair of hands'.

Panel saw This saw is needed for precision cutting, mitres and ripping timber down.

Sandpaper These come in different grades and are used for removing rough edges and splinters on timber. **Spanners and grips** These are used to tighten bolts and nuts on posts and framework, as well as for holding and fastening plumbing work. **Tin snips and metal files** The file is used to burr edges on metal and bamboo while the tin snips are for cutting sheet metals.

Try square This set square is used to check and mark right angles on timber. **Wood chisel and mallet** The wood chisel is used for cutting out joints, tidying corners and splitting bamboo. A rubber mallet can also be used in conjunction with this type of chisel.

Power tools

Cordless screwdriver This is ideal for outdoor use, as it has a rechargeable battery that does away with the need for a cumbersome cable while you are working outside. It makes fixing and undoing screws a painless job.
Jigsaw These can now be cordless as well as mains powered and are used

for cutting sheet materials such as copper and steel.
Power drill This is a drill that is specifically designed for masonry and timber, as well as concrete and blockwork. This heavy-duty drill can run off a generator or be plugged into the mains.

Tools to hire

Angle grinder This machine is in fact a petrol stone cutter. When hiring it request that you are provided with a diamond blade. The instructions for attaching the blade will be given to you by the hire company.
Chainsaw For cutting sleepers the chainsaw is fantastic, but there are strict regulations if you wish to hire one – protective clothing must be worn at all times. Listen carefully to the guidelines and rules given to you.

Concrete mixer A mixer makes mixing concrete and mortar much easier than it would be by hand. A small stand mixer is ideal. These can be petrol or electric – the electric option is quieter and therefore much more neighbour-friendly.

pools and ponds

planning for pools and ponds

There are few gardens that are too small to benefit from a natural pond or formal pool. A simple birdbath, for example, can transform a small corner of a courtyard into an area of activity as birds queue to wash and drink on a hot summer afternoon. And any still pool, however small, will reflect its surroundings and capture the pure essence of water, captivating the viewer.

Function and style It is hard to put a finger on the benefits of a body of water in the garden. Nature and children are irresistibly drawn to it – just look at children playing in puddles after a downpour. Pools can be used to calm a busy, small urban garden or to reflect architecture and planting.

The distinct difference between styles of ponds and pools relates to the formality and informality of their shape, material selection and positioning. Ultimately, the style of the feature will depend on its surroundings and your personal taste. Buildings, materials and existing features will often make the choice of style less difficult as you will want to use a sympathetic feature. Take a look at the garden's ground levels to pick up clues – a flat site will suit low-level simple pools whereas undulating surfaces provide you with the ideal opportunity to have fun with a small waterfall falling into a lagoon-style natural pond.

Design choices The key to designing the right pool is to consider the site and surrounding areas. Firstly, think about where you would like to position the water feature. The closer it is to the house, the more influence the building will have on its materials, shape and overall feel. This will usually mean that the controlled, clean lines of formal designs, which are dominated by materials and architecture, are the most suitable. The further away the pool is positioned from the building, the less control it has over the design. This gives you the opportunity to work more with curvilinear designs, and allows you to soften edges and introduce lush planting for a supportive role, providing shelter for wildlife.

Not all small gardens need formal water designs. If the site is long and narrow, simply screen off the last few

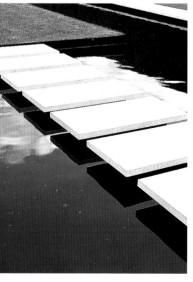

Contemporary pathway across a pool.

Spiky plants add interest.

Gravel edging creates texture.

Low planting softens a pool's edge.

To make the most of natural water areas, create an outdoor living area using decking to surround the water (top left). Enhance the fusion effect with strategically placed plants or steps (top right). On the other hand, if your goal is to create a sense of movement within the tranquillity of a pond, insert a vertical sculpture (above) that will add beauty and a three-dimensional effect to your water feature.

This modest pool incorporates striking cobbles, which have been laid on its floor, and it is also offset beautifully by the dense planting around its edge.

metres or feet to create a place of mystery. Add a seat, small pool and pump and you have a place for contemplation.

The shape and contents of the site will strongly influence your choices. Unless you plan to alter the garden dramatically by ripping out most of its contents, you will need to work with what is already there. And unless trees totally dominate and oppress the site, you should try to keep the odd one in place, as trees add maturity to a garden. Pruning will improve the shape of a tree, which can then be uplit to create an exciting backdrop.

If reflection is your aim, take time to position the pool, checking with a mirror to view it from every angle. If the pool is to be formal, without planting, it is likely that you will need some form of filter to keep the clarity and reflective quality of the water. So, assess where it would be best placed and how it can be screened off.

A small, straight, rectangular site will be best left open with the pool located centrally. This is because any body of water will dominate this type of garden, so you might as well make it the star attraction. If, however, the garden is large and full, the feature will act as a calming foil. It is almost impossible to make a still body of water too big for a plot, so build as big as your budget and site will

Ultimately, the style of the feature will depend on its surroundings and your personal taste.

allow. The larger the volume of water, the better chance it has of a natural ecology, which will keep it clean.

Curved and/or divided-up sites give the opportunity for intrigue and surprise as you can move people through different moods within the site. For example, it can be wonderful to come across a little oasis surrounded by ferns and mosses beneath a light-filtering tree.

When building a natural feature, the use of a liner to waterproof the excavations is now almost taken for granted. This is due to its ability to follow a curve and also because it saves money. Rock, cobbles, driftwood and timber edging work well to make the feature blend in with nature. If it is a natural pond that you are after, take a look at the real thing by visiting parks, lakes and lowland areas and take plenty of reference photographs.

Numerous materials and products are available to construct contemporary pools. A small metallic glazed pot will give your water feature a 'funky' style. In a gloomy courtyard, a stainless steel-clad raised pool with mirror mosaics on the base will bring the garden to life.

The projects on the following pages give an idea of how pools and ponds can be included in a garden landscape, and provide various styles and materials that are suitable for use in most gardens.

The edges of a pool or pond are just as important as the feature itself. The right surroundings can soften the effect as well as enhance the overall design. Using planting, you can create a very 'natural' feel (above left). Harder materials such as brick (above right) provide a more definite, formal edging and can be offset with other materials. Here, brick is complemented by loose gravel and the effect is completed with a modern concrete bowl positioned right at the water's edge.

The tranquil reflection of planting.

Simple brick edging.

Modern timber, pebbles and block edging.

Waterlilies help oxygenate water.

traditional
BRICK POOL

A traditional pool is one of the most essential features in a formal garden. This beautiful stock brick pool, incorporating York stone coping, is a classic design. The statement it makes is one of character and craftsmanship.

MATERIALS

Bricks

Road mesh

Cement and ballast

Wall ties

Concrete blocks

Coping stones

Conduit

Fibre-reinforced render

Bitumen paint

Pumps and filter

Marginal plants

TOOLS

Groundwork tools

Building tools

Angle grinder

Soft brush

1   On a level piece of ground mark out the area for your pool using the 3, 4, 5 method (see page 14). Then dry lay the bricks, making sure that you include 10mm ($\frac{1}{2}$in) joints along the string lines to determine the size of the pool. This will mean you can avoid cutting any bricks when you construct the wall, saving both time and money. Now lay sand lines 100mm (4in) behind your dry brick edging.

2   Bang a peg into the area around the pool about 500mm (1$\frac{3}{4}$ft) away from your pool edge. Knock it down to the finished ground level (this may be shingle, paving or whatever you choose). This peg is your datum level, which you will relate all other levels to. From this peg you will need to place another in the pool area 75mm (3in) lower down – this will be the height of your concrete base. This allows you to lay slabs up to the pool walls without the foundation concrete overlap getting in the way.

1 Lay sand lines approximately 100mm (4in) behind your dry brick edging to indicate where you should begin your excavations.

2 Once you have positioned your datum peg, you then need to add another level peg inside the pool, 75mm (3in) lower down.

KNOW YOUR MATERIALS

Bricks: Second-hand stocks have been used here, but these are only really suitable for areas with mild weather conditions. If your garden has heavy and prolonged frosts a different choice may be needed. Builder's merchants are always a good place to get advice from. As a rule, most bricks are fine for landscaping but sand-faced flettons should be avoided, as the surface tends to deteriorate through frost quickly.

Coping stones: Although York stone has been used here other natural stone is widely available. Natural stone will always look and weather better than concrete, but many substitutes look remarkably similar and cost much less.

Bang in a series of pegs to this lower level at 1m (3ft) intervals, which you will use to check the depth of your foundation (it should be 150mm/6in deep).

3 | Now cut and lay the road mesh, which strengthens the slab and prevents cracking. It is often necessary to strengthen concrete foundations to prevent ground movement destabilizing the structure. The mesh should be in the middle of the depth of the concrete slab for maximum strength so place a series of house bricks under the mesh to keep it at the correct height. Mix your foundation concrete (see page 12) and pour it over the mesh into the pool base. Tip out the concrete from the wheelbarrow; don't shovel it in until you have nearly reached up to the finished base height.

Tamp down the concrete using a float and then check it with a spirit level. The tamping action is important as it removes any bubbles. Tap down the level pegs 50mm (2in) and fill over them with concrete. Cover the base for about 48 hours to cure.

4 | Build up the first corner of the brickwork using a 1:6 mortar mix to six courses high. Pay constant attention to the mortar joints (which should be 10mm/¹⁄₂in) and level the courses as you go. When you finish the corner, rub over the mortar joints with a small piece of garden hose to produce an attractive finish. Repeat this process with the other three corners. Using the 1.2m (4ft) spirit level raise the infill brickwork up to the finished height of the corners. Include two galvanized wall ties for bonding the inside block wall on top of the third course, at a minimum of 600mm (2ft) from the corners. Repeat this process along the other three sides. Finish the mortar and brush the brickwork. Clean any excess mortar on the inside of the wall then cover the pool and allow it to cure overnight.

5 | Uncover the pool and begin the blockwork and planting shelf. Lay the first course of blockwork (using the same mortar mix) around the inside of all four sides. Make sure that the blocks are 10mm (¹⁄₂in) away from the brick skin and use a spirit level to lay them flush with the top of the

3 *Once the reinforcing mesh is in place, you should tip the concrete mix into the area and then tamp it down.*

4 *Start the brickwork by laying one corner only, which should be six courses high. Make sure you use a 1:6 mortar mix.*

5 *As you are laying the blockwork you can also lay some blocks flat in order to build up your planting shelf.*

third course of the outside brick wall. Then fill the void between the blocks and brickwork with leftover mortar. Lay the final course of blocks to the finished level with the top of the brickwork and fill the joint between the walls with mortar. Smooth with the back of a trowel. The planting shelf can also be laid at this time – simply build two courses of blocks laid flat to give depth to the shelf. Cover the pool and let it cure overnight.

6   The coping stones can now be laid. They need to overlap 50mm (2in) either side of the pool wall. The stones should be about 300–350mm (1–1¼ft) wide. It is useful to dry lay them first so start at a corner and lay one stone. Then lay the others around the edge, leaving a 10–20mm (½–¾in) pointing joint. You will probably need to cut a stone down to fit the final gap on each side using an angle grinder. Now decide where the pump cable will exit the pool and place a 10mm (½in) conduit along the wall.

Lay the corner stones using a 1:4 mortar mix, checking the level, then add the other stones. Use a straightedge to line up the overlapping edge then run a pointing trowel along the bed joint to clean off any excess mortar. Point the joints the following day with a dryish 1:3 mortar mix and brush off the stones with a soft brush.

7   The inside of the pool can be rendered using a fibre-reinforced sand and cement to improve its strength and reduce the chance of leaks. Apply the render at a thickness of around 10mm (½in). After 48 hours paint two coats of bitumen paint over it.

8   Now fit the pump. To prevent silt and debris clogging it up, place it on bricks or a concrete block. Attach an extension pipe to the pump so it is 50mm (2in) above the coping stones. Ensure the pump cable is vertical and attach it to the brickwork. It can then run into ducting laid under the surrounding area and on to the mains supply.

Fill the pool up and check the height of your fountain by adjusting the pump flow rate. Then add your chosen marginal plants to the pool (see page 18).

6 Lay the coping stones on the wall, making sure that you leave space for pointing joints. A piece of copper pipe laid in the space can help.

7 After the render has been allowed to dry, paint over its surface with two coats of waterproofing liquid.

8 Pull the cable tight and then attach it to the brickwork. It can then run into ducting to reach the mains supply.

wet and
DRY POOL

The wet and dry pool is a modern piece of contemporary art. Its angular shell, made from steel, houses a still, calm body of water that is dramatically reflective. This design needs no complications – it should just stand alone.

MATERIALS

Mirror

Hardcore

Soft sand

Steel pool and centre unit

Metal paint

Porphyry stone

Sharp sand

Cement

Pump and filters

Silicone sealant

Hoses and fittings

TOOLS

Groundwork tools

Building tools

Workbench

Angle grinder

Sealant gun

1   This feature will need to be kept perfectly level even when it is full to the brim. It will also weigh a substantial amount so it is important to provide a sturdy base. Check the position and orientation of the feature before you excavate. As it is a reflection pool, you will need to make sure that the subject you wish to reflect will be seen from the preferred viewing angle. You can check this by using a mirror laid on the ground. When you are happy with its final position, mark out your proposed base to the exact size of the pool using the 3, 4, 5 method (see page 14).

2   Now excavate the base down to a depth of 100mm (4in) below ground level, ensuring that the sides are clean and upright. To produce a level base, simply bang in timber pegs 25mm (1in) down from the surrounding ground. Place them slightly in from each corner and check that they are level using a spirit level.

1 Use the 3, 4, 5 method to mark out the proposed base and then follow along the string with sand to create sand lines.

2 Excavate the hole and then bang in timber pegs to produce a level guide for your base. You should use a spirit level to check them.

KNOW YOUR MATERIALS

UV and filter: The pool should be positioned so that the inlet and outlet holes and pipework point away from the main direction the pool will be viewed from. The edge of a border or in front of a planted wall or boundary would give the ideal environment for the pool. The UV unit and filter need to be placed above the pool, in a position that provides a measurement of at least 450mm (1½ft) between the outlet hole in the pool and the outlet at the bottom of the filter unit. Remember when positioning these that you will need regular access for maintenance so when you come to disguise the view make sure you allow room for access.

3   Fill the hole up to ground level with hardcore. When the hardcore has been compacted it will allow room for a thin layer of sand, which is needed to create a level platform for the pool to sit on. To compact it, use a hand rammer and work from one side across the whole square, ramming the hardcore down into the base. When you have finished the area, go over it once more in the opposite direction, ensuring any holes are filled and bumps taken out (roughly check it with a spirit level).

4   You now need to paint both parts of the pool with black metal paint. First make sure that they are free from dust and water. Then place them on a workbench or covered table as it is important to be comfortable when painting these (it will take a couple of hours). Paint the inside and outside of both pools and leave them protected with plastic sheeting for 24 hours to dry before handling again.

5   Once the pools are dry the stones that make up the central feature of the pool can be laid in the smaller of the two steel units. It is likely that the stones will need cutting to fit exactly so use an angle grinder.

Mark down from the top of the unit the depth of the stones minus 20mm ($^3/_4$in) – this is the height the infill material will be, allowing for compaction. Fill the unit up to this line with a dryish 1:6 cement and sharp sand mix. Using a rubber hammer (or the handle of a club hammer), tap each stone down until it is level with the top of the unit. Repeat this process until they are all in place. It is a good idea, if you are building this alone, to work in a wheelbarrow. The unit will be very heavy when completed so if it is already in a barrow you only have to lift it once into the pool.

6   The pool needs to sit very level in its final position, so a thin screed is laid over the compacted hardcore. Spread a layer of sharp sand over the top of the hardcore base to a depth of 25mm (1in). Then, with the use of the spirit level and float, flatten the sand to produce the base for the pool. Ask for help to lift the pool into position, making

3 Once you have filled up the area with hardcore you need to compact it down. Do this by using a hand rammer.

4 Place both parts of the pool onto a workbench and then paint both the insides and outsides of them with black metal paint.

5 Place the stones into position in the smaller unit and tap them down so that they are level with the top using a rubber mallet.

sure that the holes for the pipes are facing the least viewed area of the garden. Gently lower it into place, ensuring that you do not drop one side quicker than the other. Then check if any adjustments are needed by placing a spirit level across the top of the pool from side to side. Then lift the small steel unit with the stones into the steel pool. Position the stone unit into place by eye then check it is centralized by measuring between the unit and all the pool sides.

7   Now fit the pump, positioning it on the opposite side to the inlet hole in the side of the pool. This will ensure that the whole body of water is cleaned, not just around the inlet hole. Lay the cable for the pump neatly around the inside edge of the pool and then pass it through the pre-drilled hole next to the inlet and seal around the cable using clear silicone sealant. When you choose the position for the feature, it is important to take into account how you will disguise the filter and UV system. They need to be on a secure base (e.g. a timber platform)

and it is important that they are kept higher than the pool as gravity feeds the water back into the pool.

Once the filter and UV clarifier are in place, measure the distance of hose from the pump to the UV unit, cut and fit it using a jubilee clip (remember that this needs to pass through the pre-cut hole next to the power cable hole). Next measure and cut a pipe for the return journey from the filter and fix this to the side of the pool, fitting a filter cone over the end. Make sure you leave enough for the pipe to protrude into the pool. Now connect the pump, UV and filter following the manufacturer's recommendations (see also page 17 for general guidelines on safely installing pumps).

8   Finally, you can fill the pool with water. It is best to doublecheck the levels of the unit one last time before you do this, as it will be almost impossible to move the pool when it is filled with water. Once the pool is full the pump can be switched on and the connections and joints checked for leaks.

6 Carefully lift and position the central stone unit into its final resting place inside the steel pool. Then check that it is centred.

7 Now connect all the pipework for the filters and install the pump. The pump should be on the opposite side to the inlet hole.

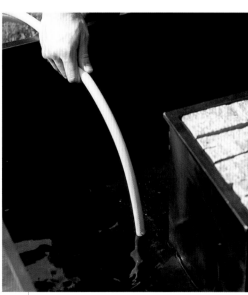

8 Once you have done one last check to see that the unit is level, fill it up with water using a garden hose.

spiral POOL

The spiral pool has the calm serenity of a natural body of water. Its interest lies in the pattern that you create within the pool, whether a formal geometric design or following a more organic style – the choice is yours.

1 | Choose the area in the garden for your pool – you will need at least a 3 x 3m (10 x 10ft) plot of relatively flat soil. Take a steel pin or bamboo cane and push it into the centre of the plot. Then, using a string line that is marked with the correct radius or a builder's tape placed over the cane or pin, rotate it around the central cane laying sand as you go at a radius of 1.2m (4ft). Lay the sand around the circle until it is complete; this will give the markings for a pool with a diameter of 2.4m (8ft). Bang in and level a series of pegs around the circumference to give you a reference after you have finished your excavations.

2 | Now remove the cane and begin the excavations. The idea is to create a shallow pan that gently slopes to a depth of 400mm (1¼ft). Once the main pan has been dug out, a central sump hole measuring 600mm (2ft) wide and 400mm (1¼ft) deep will need to be excavated. This

MATERIALS

Steel pin or bamboo cane

Soft sand

Fleece underlay

Butyl liner

Pump and filter

Hoses and fittings

Road mesh

Membrane

Chicken wire

Crushed slate

White cobbles

Conduit

TOOLS

Groundwork tools

Building tools

Gloves

1 Rotate your tape once you have measured the correct radius and, as you do so, lay sand to create an entire circle.

2 After you have excavated the main pool, dig out the central sump hole. This will eventually contain the pump.

KNOW YOUR MATERIALS

Slate: When ordering the slate from your local stone supplier be aware that you need to order at least one week before you need it. You may also incur a small delivery charge as it generally comes in 1 tonne (1cwt) bags. If access is a problem and the stone cannot be easily placed next to the pool, then purchasing 40kg (88lb) bags may be the answer as these are easier to carry or wheel barrow around to the site of the pool.

Stone: During the quarrying process all stone will naturally attract a layer of dust and dirt. Therefore it is important to wash all pebbles and cobbles thoroughly prior to placing them in or around your water feature.

hole will contain the pump that will slowly move the water to a filter system, which is needed to keep the water clear.

Start the main excavation from the edges and gradually grade it down to the centre. Keep standing back to check the evenness of your work and, when you are happy with the overall shape of the pool, check the surrounding edges are level with the pegs. You will need to excavate the central sump hole, paying attention to the sides to keep them upright with the walls intact.

3 | Before you lay the protective fleece, remove any large stones or sharp objects from the pool. Lay the fleece over the whole area and, starting in the sump hole, carefully fold the material into the hole. Then work your way out to the edge of the pool, keeping folds to an absolute minimum.

4 | Now place the butyl liner over the pool and fold it into the sump hole. The liner needs to be 3.5 × 3.5m (11 1/2 ×

11 1/2ft). Start by laying the liner over one side of the pool. You should remove your footwear so you do not rip or puncture the liner. Next, fold the liner into the sump hole. Do not worry about any resulting small folds as the liner will be covered with the slate. Continue to fit the liner over the rest of the pool until it is complete.

5 | Place the pump into the sump hole in the middle of the pool. Then attach the hose to the pump outlet fastening it with a jubilee clip. Now the hose and power cable need to be positioned flat against the liner so that the crushed slate can disguise them. The hose will need a flow adjuster to control the quantity of water flowing into the filter (see page 17). This needs to be situated at the edge of the pool for access, but can be disguised later.

You now need to place a grill over the sump hole. Using bolt croppers, cut a grill measuring 1m² (3ft²) out of a sheet of road mesh before positioning it. Also cut four lengths of membrane about 1.1m (3 1/4ft) in length – these will be the cushioning for the grill over the sump hole.

3 The protective fleece liner can be laid in place once you have removed any large stones and debris.

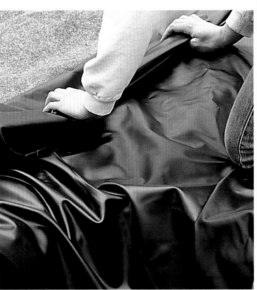

4 Carefully lay the liner over the hole. Remove your shoes when you do this to reduce the risk of tearing the liner.

5 Once the grill is in place you can add a layer of chicken wire over the top, which is needed for the slate to sit on.

Place the membrane on the liner so that it will lay under the sharp edges of the grill, then place the grill carefully over the sump hole. Finally a layer of expanded metal or chicken wire is needed to allow the slate to lie over the top without the stones falling through.

6 | Next cover the whole pool area with a membrane. This will protect the liner from the sharp slate and will also provide a barrier to prevent the pump being clogged up with silt and sediment. Wearing gloves, wash and then lay the slate over the pool at a depth of 50mm (2in), trying to keep it as even and flat as possible. When it is completely covered, take a step back so that you can make sure there is no membrane showing through.

7 | You can now fill the pool with water. The level that you fill the pool up to will depend on the height of the cobbles that you have laid. As long as these are covered then the water level is adequate. Now connect the pump, ensuring that all cabling is ducted in rigid plastic conduit

450–600mm (1 1/2–2ft) below ground level until it reaches the switch box. Turn the pump on and adjust the filtration unit so that the flow back into the pool does not disturb the view of the pool.

Using washed white cobbles, the pattern can now be laid out on the bottom of the pool. Start from a central point with a large cobble and then lay a continuous line of stones, unravelling the shape until you have completed your spiral. When you have laid them all out, stand back and decide where you feel you need to alter the shape or width of the cobble lines. Try to use stones of similar size for this and lay them as flat as possible.

Alternative materials

In this feature crushed slate and white cobbles were used to provide a stunning contrast of colours and give depth to the otherwise shallow pool. There are other materials that could be used to line the pool such as crushed glass or coloured aggregate. The pattern that you decide on can echo themes that already exist in your garden.

6 Once the membrane is in position, lay the washed slate over the whole pool, wearing gloves to protect your hands.

7 Create your spiral pattern for the bottom of the pool.. Work from the centre outwards, checking the pattern as you go.

Alternative materials: There are many other materials you could use to line your pool, such as glass or coloured aggregate.

natural POND

The natural pond is the most commonly built feature in domestic gardens and it is easy to see why. An antidote to our fast-moving world, the pond reconnects us to nature and wildlife and provides a focal point for calm and relaxation in the garden.

1 Choose the area where you want the pond to be positioned and mark the shape on the ground using sand. Drive a reference peg into the ground just outside the sand line – this will indicate all of your levels. Drive in pegs every 1m (3ft) or so around the remainder of the sand line down to just above ground level. Check these are the same height by using your spirit level and, if needed, a straightedge. On the outside of the sand line (i.e. not the pond area) remove the turf or soil to a depth of 50mm (2in) and a width of 300mm (1ft). If you want to put the turf back as a natural edge to the pond at the end then lay it out in the garden and keep it well watered.

2 Excavate down within the sand line to a depth of 250mm (10in) from ground level, using pegs to check that you have excavated to the correct depth. Rake over the surface and remove any large stones or debris from the

MATERIALS

Soft sand

Fleece underlay

Butyl liner

Bricks and slab

Pumps and accessories

TOOLS

Groundwork tools

Building tools

1 Drive in a reference peg every 1m (3ft) along the sand line and use your spirit level to check that they are at the same height.

2 Once you have excavated the deep part of the pond out, rake over the bottom in order to ensure that no large stones are left in.

KNOW YOUR MATERIALS

If nature is to be encouraged then hundreds of Koi carp and plastic flamingos will not make the ideal setting. A natural pond needs to be about creating an environment for wildlife. The body of water should have the right planting and leave room for nature.

Edging: This can change the feel of the pond and its function. A wildlife pond may need no hard edging at all. If you back the lawn up to the water's edge, and mix this with surrounding planting, you can create the feel of a natural environment for wildlife. A York stone or slate edging will, alternatively, create a definite frame to the pond. This provides a focus on the planting within the pond.

site. Now mark out the deep area of the pond. You will need to leave a marginal shelf around the edge of the top of the pond for planting. Measure in from the sides of the pool 300mm (1ft) then lay a sand line as before to mark out the shape to be excavated for the deep part of the pond. Excavate the inside of the sand line down to a depth of 400mm (1¼ft), then rake the bottom over to check for sharp or large stones.

Due to the pressure of the water being greatest at the bottom of the pond, you will need to make a 50mm (2in) layer of either sifted soil or soft sand to help cushion the liner, which will ensure that it doesn't get punctured.

3   Next, lay the fleece underlay over the pond and work it into the edges and contours of the pond. Push the fleece into its position firmly. As you do this, try not to lean or stand on the planting shelves. When the fleece is in place, trim the edges off it using a craft knife or scissors. Make sure you leave a small overlap going over onto the edge of the surrounding soil.

4   Roll the liner out over the top of the pond. Push the liner roughly into the shape of the pond and use bricks to hold the edges of the liner in place temporarily. When the liner is ready for filling with water the pump can be positioned on two bricks, which have a small slab on top of them, in the deep part of the pond. Then position the power cable along the inside of the pond to where you wish it to pass under the edging. The water needs to be passed through the pump to stop it from stagnating. Once the pond has been planted up, the plants will take care of the oxygenation and also provide shade.

5   Fill the pond up slowly with water. The liner will spread into the contours of the pond with the increasing weight of the water. As the pond fills up you will need to fold or pleat the larger parts of the liner into place. Remember to adjust the bricks on the edges as the liner becomes taut.

6   Once the pond is nearly full you can check the edges for level using the water line as a guide. Simply adjust the soil

3 Place the fleece underlay over the pool and then, taking care not to lean on the planting shelves, work it into the edges.

4 Once the underlay has been positioned and cut, you can then roll the liner out over the top of the pond.

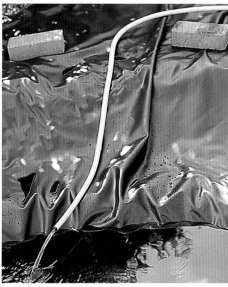

5 Begin to fill the pond with water. The liner will naturally spread into the corners of the pond but you will need to adjust the bricks.

levels behind the liner to provide a consistent level edge. You will then need to excavate a trench 150mm (6in) deep around the pond to tuck the liner into. This also produces an edge that can be planted up to, which looks pleasing to the eye.

With the edges completed, trim the liner more accurately using a sharp knife or scissors. Then backfill the trench and gently firm the soil down with your heel. Rake this over to produce a medium tilth for plants or turf.

7 The power cable from the pump needs to be at a safe depth of 450mm (1½ft) to protect it from tools and animals etc. So, from the conduit exiting the pool, run the rest of the cable in the same protective tubing until it reaches the connection point.

8 Now that the edges are tidy you can plant or turf right up to the pool. If you choose to turf, it is preferable to use the grass that was stripped out when you cleared the site. This is because it will blend in far better than new grass

would as it will be in keeping with its surroundings. Once you have laid all your turf, firm it in using the back of a spade and then water it thoroughly until it becomes established. It is often best to let the grass grow longer around natural ponds as this softens edges and provides extra protection and habitat for wildlife.

Now a recirculating pump can be connected and switched on. The power connection from the pump needs to be carried out by a qualified electrician.

If after a few weeks your water turns green use a pump with a simple oxygenating tube attachment. This will help your pond in the first few seasons while the plants become established.

Alternative materials

You may prefer to use a hard edging, such as York stone or slate, rather than turf. This provides a safe edge for inquisitive children. For this reason, it is important to bed the stone correctly on a minimum of 75mm (3in) ratio of 1:4 cement and sharp sand.

6 When the pond is full and the liner has become taut, you should trim the edges. Check the height of the liner using the water.

7 Power cables always need to be protected so run your cable in conduit underneath the paving and on to the connection point.

8 If you decide to dress the edge of the pond with lawn, you can re-lay the turf that you removed when excavating the pond area.

streams and rills

planning for streams and rills

A natural stream will always fascinate and inspire, providing hours of calm meditation as you follow the path the water takes over and around rocks, boulders and planting. In contrast, rills are formal features that demonstrate control and precision. Rills originated out of the need to tame nature and direct this valuable, natural resource to irrigate pastures. In a garden setting, this style of feature allows you to create modern design with real impact.

Function and style Put simply, the difference between a stream and a rill lies in the overall style – a stream is natural while a rill is manmade. Both can be termed as watercourses, as they are a means of channelling or moving a body of water from an outlet to a reservoir or ornamental pool. The key to creating an authentic, 'natural' stream is the ability to emulate nature. Attention must be paid to the way water unpredictably gushes and then suddenly dissipates – this effect is often difficult to achieve in modern-day garden plots. It can also be hard to break from the domination of the house so natural streams are more appropriate in larger gardens where they can be placed far from the house, or where there is some sort of a physical barrier such as a screen. This will allow you to create a naturalistic environment.

Formality and geometry are characteristics associated with rills and small channels. These water features tend to be straight and fairly narrow – mainly due to the difficulty and expense of constructing curved and sinuous shapes through terraces or paving. The straighter shapes are also far more in keeping with more modern architecture, giving an ideal opportunity to bring water close to a house. You can create cohesion by linking the materials of the rill with those used for the house or the existing components of a patio. For example, stone or brick can be used to form the edges of the feature. Alternatively, if your property lacks a strong period style try using more contemporary materials such as steel, glass, concrete and mosaics.

Design choices Your site will, to a certain extent, dictate the type of feature that is most suitable and it will also give you clues to the design and choice of materials that should be used. A sloping area, for example, provides

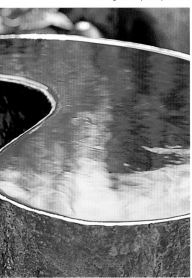

An organically shaped rill.

Core-ten steel slabs with a steel-sided rill.

A formal rill edged with stone.

A winding rill leads to a pond.

Whether manmade or natural, a passageway of water can be highlighted or softened by using planting. When creating a 'natural', meandering stream, informal, dense and overhanging plants can add to the effect (top left). And placing a walkway over the top adds yet another dimension. You may choose to create a traditional bridge (above) or a more adventurous 'stepping stone' using pieces of timber (top right) – either way you will be able to enjoy the view from above.

This shallow pool empties into an angular rill. The strong shapes used in the design are softened by surrounding gravel and planting.

the ideal opportunity to introduce an exciting series of falls that add noise and animation to the water's journey (see pages 72–5). In natural stream design the rapid change of level of a small waterfall is often followed by stillness as the body of water re-groups to continue its passage. This can easily be achieved by excavating a mini-pool directly beneath the fall to increase the volume of water and absorb the kinetic energy of the turbulent water. It is often this stop-and-start characteristic of a stream that gives a sense of natural movement. Without it, the stream could become a rather one-dimensional, single run of water.

Arching and overhanging trees and shrubs provide a vertical dimension, linking the horizontal elements of the water with its surroundings. A bridge, on the other hand, is a wonderful way of experiencing the feature in a more intimate manner, as it allows you to see a totally different, close-up view of your creation. Stepping stones are another great way to interact with the water – children will love moving across a stream in this way.

Look to nature and study the way it creates its streams. Pay attention to the way rocks are almost dropped into the middle of a stream. This indicates the power of water and should be a useful guide to where you should position your

The key to creating an authentic 'natural' stream is the ability to emulate nature.

final boulders. Nature, over time, also grades sand, gravel and rock so avoid using a lot of the same-sized material.

The strong geometry of a rill can be difficult to introduce successfully into the garden. The dominance of a straight line naturally draws attention and creates strong directional movement, leading the eye to its end. You can take advantage of this by terminating the rill with a focal point, such as an elegant water jet in the centre of a low-level pool. You may want to dissect an area of your garden by using the rill or link a relaxing seating terrace through to a wilder area. With all this in mind, take your time when positioning the feature. Mark out the rill with sand then look at the overall balance of the area and check that you can still use the connecting areas as you want to.

A rill, by its very nature, is the middle section of a water feature – the beginning, or outlet, can be as simple as a stone covering a hose or an elaborate series of spouts feeding the channel. The channel itself can be transformed by decorating the bottom with shells, pebbles, glass etc. The destination, or reservoir, should suit the overall style.

The following projects incorporate all these design principles and provide you with details of construction techniques to enable you to create the perfect stream or rill for your garden.

In a large garden, you can create a very natural-looking stream that reflects the ground contours and blends in with the natural environment (top left). However, a stream or rill does not need to take up so much space. A small, self-contained feature that includes a reservoir and watercourse to emulate the flow of a river can be just as effective (top right). This even adds an abstract art dimension to the garden too and will probably become a talking point among visitors.

A timber walkway over a stream.

Slate covers the bottom of this stream.

Dramatic planting beside a stream.

Cobbles line this straight rill.

copper RILL

Nestled among the natural textured sleepers runs this inviting and colourful copper rill. The elements of water and metal combine here to reflect the light and provide a focal point.

1 This feature should be a minimum of seven sleepers wide (about 1.75m/5¾ft). First decide how wide your deck needs to be in relation to the overall area you are installing. Measure the width of a sleeper and multiply it until you get as close as possible to the required site width. Now construct the outside frame using 75 × 50mm (3 × 2in) treated timber. It should be constructed smaller than the final deck size so that the sleepers will overlap the frame by 50mm (2in) on each side. Check the frame is square by using a builders' square and nail it together using 100mm (4in) galvanized nails. Then fix intermediate timbers at 1.2m (4ft) intervals. Lay the frame in its proposed site and mark the position of all the timbers using sand. Then put it aside.

2 The foundation blocks should be laid on 75–100mm (3–4in) of 1:3 sharp sand and cement. Work from the

1 Once you have decided how big your framework needs to be, construct it and fix it together using galvanized nails.

2 Once the corner foundation blocks are in place, your frame on top of them to check that they align correctly with all its corners.

KNOW YOUR MATERIALS

Copper: Although copper can look a little new and glittery, verdigris quickly forms on it to calm down the reflection and give character to the metal. Copper has a unique quality when it is used alongside such natural and earthy materials as wood and water because the effect is always rich and satisfying. Some alternative materials can create a modern, clean and refreshing look. Stainless steel can expand light in a shady garden, reflecting the purity of running water. Copper has the advantage of being relatively easy to bend and work with while stainless steel is a little more resilient, needing a specialist fabricator to produce the shapes and bends.

corner of the frame and level around using a straightedge and a spirit level. Once the corner blocks are in position, carefully sit the frame onto the blocks and adjust them if necessary so that they sit flush with the outside corners. The intermediate blocks can be laid at 1.2m (4ft) intervals along the outside frame and internal timbers. Check their position after they are laid by placing the made-up frame over the blocks again. Leave the blocks to set overnight.

3 Fit a membrane underneath your framework and pin it down with wire loops or spread a 50mm (2in) layer of gravel over the area. Having covered the soil, set your sleepers in their final position and check the overlap of the frame on each side. Measure the opening for the rill and adjust each end to form a parallel channel then mark the frame underneath for reference when fixing. Next, fix the sleepers using 100mm (4in) galvanized nails.

4 Whether you are using an existing pump in the reservoir or are connecting a new one, the hose will carry the water up to the outlet at the top of the rill. Make sure your connections to the pump from the hose are tight using a jubilee clip. Then, in order to feed the hose under the deck area, ensure that the hose has ample length at each end (about 1m/3ft). If you are using a lined pool, cut a small hole just under the frame timber and push the pipe hose through this, to lay the hose under the rill opening. Positioning the hose here will allow you easy access to it in the future.

5 Now attach a timber fascia to the frame directly under the sleepers. This covers the hose entry point and also hides the liner upstand. When filled, the water line should be 25–50mm (1–2in) from the bottom of this timber, which makes an attractive water edge and a good indicator of when the pool may need topping up. Prior to fixing, paint the 150 x 25mm (6 x 1in) treated timber with black timber preservative and allow it to dry for 12 hours. Screw the boards to the frame using 75mm (3in) zinc-coated screws as high up to the sleeper as you can.

3 Once you have put a membrane over the ground, put the sleepers in place and fix them with galvanized nails.

4 Feed the hose that takes water to the outlet at the top of the rill under the deck area, ensuring there is ample length at either end.

5 Paint the timber fascia with black preservative before attaching it directly under the sleepers using zinc-coated screws.

6 Now start to form the copper rill. Measure the width of the opening and add the two sides to the measurement – this will give your copper strip width. When deciding the length allow 150mm (6in) for the chute at the front and 150mm (6in) extra if you need more than one length of copper. This will provide an overlap for fixing two sheets together (to fix simply silicone and lay one sheet over the previous one, working up the rill).

Wearing gloves, mark the width of the sheet (the rill opening plus two upstands of 110mm/4½in). Then, using a high-quality pair of tin snips or a jigsaw fitted with a metal blade, cut along the lengths. Once this has been done, the upstands can be bent into shape. Mark the height of the sleeper (around 100mm/4¼in) at each end of the sheet and line up these marks with the edge of a piece of timber. Slowly bend the copper along its length to form a right angle. Repeat the process on the other side.

7 At one end of the rill measure back along 150mm (6in) and mark it with a felt tip pen. Then mark down 40mm (1½in) from the top of the upstand with a set square. With sharp tin snips, cut down the 40mm (1½in) you have marked, then bend this over at a right angle to the rill side. Next, measure out 30mm (1¼in) from the top edge of the bend and mark along the entire flap, leaving a 10mm (½in) right angle. Cut along the pen mark with your tin snips. Repeat this on the other side to create your water chute. Put the chute into position and nail it securely in place using small 10mm (½in) copper pins.

8 The outlet at the top of the rill needs to be constructed from one piece of copper sheet. Using a metal drill bit, drill an 18mm (¾in) hole for the tank connector to attach to. Then bend the copper over a piece of timber. The outlet should fit tightly into place, held by the sides of the fixed rill and four copper nails. Seal between the outlet and rill sides with silicone sealant, which will then need 48 hours to dry. Finally, attach the hose to the tank connector with a jubilee clip, turn the water on and make any necessary adjustments to the flow.

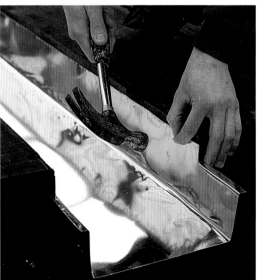

6 Once you have cut the copper to the required width, bend it along a length of timber to form a right angle for the rill.

7 Once the rill has been put in its final position in between two sleepers it can be nailed into place with copper pins.

8 Now connect the flexible hose to the tank connector using a jubilee clip. Ensure that all the connections are tight.

meandering RILL

This feature is a clever fusion of two classic forms, combining the organic shapes of the natural stream with the precision of the straight rill. The gently curving shape is reminiscent of water's natural path while the steel edge and brilliant crushed glass are thoroughly urban.

MATERIALS

Soft sand

Fleece underlay

Butyl liner

Sharp sand

Cement

150mm (6in) wide steel edging (1mm/¹/₃₀in thick)

Hoses and fittings

Two 40kg (88lb) bags of crushed glass

25mm (1in) plastic pipe

25mm (1in) plastic bend

Ballast

Pump and fittings

Granite bridge

TOOLS

Groundwork tools

Building tools

Bucket

1   This feature needs to be built at one end of an existing pool or pond, which will act as the reservoir. If you need to build a new one see page 13 for advice on construction. The rill needs to be a minimum of 5m (16ft) long, and 150mm (6in) in width. Your reservoir must be able to accommodate the amount of water needed along the meandering rill, so the longer you make the rill, the larger the amount of water you will need. With sand, mark out the passage of your rill then dig it out, making sure that its base has a gradual slope towards the existing reservoir using your spirit level.

2   Cut 1m (3ft) lengths of the fleece underlay then work out the width you need by adding the base width of the rill, the sides and an extra 200mm (8in) to allow for trimming to the necessary shape. Then lay the cut pieces into place, making sure you push them into the corners of the rill.

1 Once you have cleared the whole site and marked out your rill, begin to dig the area out using a spade.

2 Once the fleece and liner are in place, and have been folded where necessary, cut the edges, leaving a 150mm (6in) overlap.

KNOW YOUR MATERIALS

The inside of the rill is a base of sharp sand and cement. The steel sides will reflect the water's motion, and create a contemporary feel. The steel could be replaced with copper, galvanized steel or plastic. The base of the rill could also be dressed with crushed glass or flat pebbles to give a very different look. This rill is positioned in a woodland setting and bordered by natural fall from surrounding trees and shrubs. Such a rill can actually be positioned anywhere – for example in a patio leading to a pool or with a cascade trailing into your rill. There are no restrictions – the only factors that may need consideration are safety, gradient and reservoir size.

Lay the liner out over the rill and push into place, folding where necessary. Then cut the liner to fit around the edges of the rill, leaving an 150mm (6in) overlap on each side to allow for adjustment. At the edge of the reservoir, overlap the liner into the reservoir by another 150mm (6in) as this will guarantee the safe return of the water from the rill to the existing reservoir. With the fleece and liner in shape, the base of the rill can be covered in 50mm (2in) of 3:1 sharp sand and cement mix. With your level, make sure that the fall towards the reservoir is still the same on top of the sand and cement as it was on top of the liner. Use your float to create a good finish.

3 Take the lengths of 150mm (6in) wide steel and place them roughly into position inside the rill and then bend them into shape. When you are happy that all the steel sides are in their correct shapes remove them and label them so you know which position to put them back into. Store the steel safely until you are ready to set them into the sand and cement. Be sure to keep the steel sheets on their edges while they are being stored. Once they have been bent into shape they should all stay as you want them to. However, due to the thickness, if the sheets are laid flat they will lose their shape.

4 Take the steel strips and, starting from the outlet end of the rill, place them onto the mortar mix. Overlap the edges of the steel in the direction of the reservoir. With a rubber mallet or the handle of your club hammer tamp the steel into place. The top of the steel should be 25mm (1in) above ground level. Check it is all level then leave the sharp sand and cement mix to cure for 48 hours.

5 Place the pump into the reservoir inside a bucket – this will stop the pump from sucking in debris from the reservoir. Connect the hose to the outlet on the pump and secure it with a jubilee clip. Take the crushed glass and spread it around along the concrete surface of the rill. Be sure to give it an even covering – around 10–15mm (¼–¼in) should be enough to disguise the mortar floor.

3 Once you have placed the steel strips inside the rill and have bent them into their correct shapes, remove and label them.

4 Place the steel strips onto the mortar mix and then, using a rubber mallet, tamp the steel down, checking both sides are level.

5 You can now disguise the mortar bed by placing crushed glass along the rill's floor. A covering of 10–15mm (¹/₂–²/₃in) is enough.

6   The outlet needs to be fixed into place at the beginning of the rill. Cut two 100mm (4in) lengths of 25mm (1in) plastic pipe, then fit both pipes into a 90°, 25mm (1in) plastic bend. Cut and fix the flexible hose from the pump in your reservoir to reach the outlet end of the rill. Fit this to the plastic 25mm (1in) pipe with a jubilee clip.

Cut a 150mm (6in) length off one of the steel strips to form an end to the outlet of the rill. Fit this the same way you did the sides. With the end in place, fit another 90° bend to the other pipe's end. This will angle the water down into the rill, which is important to cut back on splashing.

Position the hose and the pipes so that the end of the 90° bend rests on top of the steel end that you have fitted. With this in place, concrete the area with a 1:4 mix of cement and ballast and check the pipe is central to the rill. Cover the concrete and leave it for 48 hours to cure.

7   Neatly position the hose from the pump to the outlet along one side of the rill. The pipe needs to be below the level of the mulch and against the steel. Fill the reservoir up with water. Turn the power to the pump on and observe the water flow. The flow rate may need adjusting so fiddle with the flow rate adjuster on your pump to increase or decrease the rate the water moves at. The material covering the bottom of the rill will be washed away constantly if the pressure of the outlet is too high, so this is a good indication that adjustment is needed.

8   You can now disguise the outlet by covering it with the granite bridge. This bridge will need to be positioned so that it disguises the pipework completely. The granite bridge will not need to be bedded on a mortar base, as it is purely added for aesthetic reasons and will therefore not be used as a real bridge. Depending on the material that surrounds the rill area the backfilling can be soil or forest mulch. Whichever you use, the steel needs to be a fraction higher than the surrounding area to protect it from debris. Tidy the area up and check that you are happy with the feature.

7 The hose that runs from the pump to the outlet needs to be positioned neatly along one side of the rill, below the level of the mulch.

6 *Before the cement cures, check that the pipework is in its correct position, so that it is aimed into the centre of the rill.*

8 *Once the granite bridge is in place you can add to the surrounding material. Here, mulch has been used.*

steel raised
RILL

This cool volume of shimmering water links beautifully with modern interiors. Positioned within a modern courtyard, it creates a striking feature. Alternatively, where two areas of a design meet, use this rill to divide the more formal space from a 'wilder' area.

MATERIALS

75 × 50mm (3 × 2in) treated timber

100mm (4in), 75mm (3in) and 35mm (1½in) zinc-plated screws

12mm (½in) and 9mm (⅓in) external marine ply

Protective fleece

Butyl liner

30mm (1¼in) galvanized clout nails

3 adjustable submersible pumps

Associated nozzles and extension pipes

Prefabricated stainless steel sheets

Clear external silicone sealant

Masking tape

Three bricks

TOOLS

Woodwork tools

Building tools

Staple gun

Drill

Sealant gun

Damp rag

1   The beauty of this feature is that it can be built almost entirely before being put into its final position. A basic framework of treated 75 × 50mm (3 × 2in) timber makes up the structure of the rill, which is then clad with external ply. Construct the two long sides of the rill so that they are 1.8m (6ft) long and 600mm (2ft) in height. Check the corners are 90° using a try square then fix the timbers using 75mm (3in) and 100mm (4in) zinc-plated screws. You will need to attach a central support timber to add extra stability. Now connect the two main sides with a 400mm (1¼ft) long timber top and bottom so the overall width of the ends are 500mm (1¾ft). The base of the feature will also need a support timber.

2   Once the frame has been screwed together, check each corner for square. All internal and external sides of the frame then need to be clad with marine ply, including

1 Make up the basic framework of the rill using central support timbers and fixing everything with zinc-plated screws.

2 The internal and external sides of the frame are then clad with marine ply. Attach the outside ply using screws again.

KNOW YOUR MATERIALS

Stainless steel is a versatile material, usually associated with modern interiors but it is increasingly being used outside for its clean, contemporary, hard-wearing qualities. The steel can be ordered in different grades and surface finishes. Although slightly more expensive, you should choose a marine grade, as the standard grade will develop tiny oxidized rust marks. The steel used in this feature has a brushed finish that is more suitable for exterior use as it prevents the extreme sunlight glare that is associated with the usual polished surface. It also has the added bonus of not marking as easily. To help maintain its reflective and cool appearance, regularly apply baby oil.

the base. Use 12mm ($\frac{1}{2}$in) thick for the external and 9mm ($\frac{1}{3}$in) for internal cladding. Attach the ply using 35mm (1$\frac{1}{2}$in) zinc-plated screws. Decide which end of the rill your cable will exit and leave the internal ply unscrewed to ensure ease of access for the cabling later.

3 Before you install the liner, check over the surface of the internal ply for large splinters or screwheads that may pierce the liner. A protective fleece is also laid in between the liner and internal ply for protection. Measure and cut the length and width of the fleece and liner (see page 13), adding an extra 500mm (1$\frac{3}{4}$ft) to each to allow for corner folds. Then fold the fleece into each corner and staple or nail using 30mm (1$\frac{1}{4}$in) galvanized clouts, so it is about 40mm (1$\frac{1}{2}$in) below the top of the rill. Trim the top of the fleece with a sharp blade and repeat the process for the liner. Try to ensure the liner is tucked into the corners snugly and is sitting flush on the floor of the rill or the weight of the water will pull down the liner and tear the fixing. Don't attach the materials where your cables exit.

4 Three separate pumps are used here. The pumps should each have a built-in flow valve or a flow adjuster positioned close to the pump within the nozzle extension, to adjust the volume and height of individual jets. A jet nozzle is then attached to the extension pipe.

The pump will sit on a brick at the bottom of the rill so this needs to be taken into account when cutting the length of the nozzle extension – the water line will be just above the stainless steel lip and the nozzle should sit about 30mm (1$\frac{1}{4}$in) above this.

5 Place each pump close to its final position, laying the cables along the floor of the rill. Group the cables together using cable ties. Give each pump an extra 50cm (1$\frac{1}{4}$ft) of cable in case of adjustments Using a timber fly bit, drill a hole through the top and bottom of the frame and feed the pump cables through. Re-fix the sheet and attach the fleece and liner back in position. The cables will need to be connected by a qualified electrician to a weather-proof junction box that carries the live armoured cable.

3 Once the fleece is in position to protect the liner from wood, tuck the liner in on top of it and staple it to fix it.

4 Three pumps have been used to create the fountains. They have extension pipes that need to be cut to the right length.

5 Once you have drilled your holes through the timber frame, feed the pump cables through them.

6 | The stainless steel panels can be lifted into position to check that they fit together correctly. Pay particular attention to the corners as they will be the most visible part of the rill. When you are happy, remove one of the long panels and apply a 6mm (¼in) bead of clear exterior silicone sealant in a zigzag pattern across the face of the ply. Carefully lift the panel over the top edge of the rill and lower into its final position, checking the corners are flush with the side panels and that the liner is covered. Gently slap the length of the sheet with your palm to ensure the silicone grabs hold of the steel and repeat the process on the opposite side. Then fix the steel to the remaining side panels and make sure that you leave the silicone to dry out overnight.

7 | It is important to seal and waterproof all the joints with silicone sealant so that water cannot penetrate the wooden framework. Gently pull 50mm (2in) of the protective plastic away from each joint and fix masking tape to both sides to prevent smearing silicone over the steel. Apply the clear silicone along each joint, ensuring the compound goes right into the joints. Squeeze in more sealant than you need and clean any excess off with a damp rag. Once the silicone is dry the feature is ready for its final location.

8 | The rill needs to be placed on a flat level surface, ideally on a patio. You will need some help to lift the feature to its final position, taking care not to twist the structure as this would break the seals. Once in location, check the level along its length and from front to back, adjusting where necessary using timber wedges or slate packed under the base. Place the pumps on one brick each, laid on some fleece to protect the liner.

You can now remove the plastic protection film to reveal the stainless steel. Fill the rill with water so that it finishes 40mm (1½in) down from the top of the steel lip and adjust your nozzle extension pipes so they sit just below the water line. Turn the pumps on and fine tune the flow adjusters until you are happy with the water jet.

6 Be sure to apply an evenly spaced coat of silicone sealant to the ply panel – the zigzag pattern will allow it to firmly grip onto the steel.

7 Stick the masking tape along the edge of the steel where you will be applying sealant. Now fill the small void between the steel sheets.

8 Adjust the height of the fountains with the pump flow adjusters. Do this while the water is flowing.

natural STREAM

This natural stream gives a chance for escapism, and allows nature's influence to be caught and placed in a garden. The stream's sound, movement and size make it an exciting and impressive feature.

1 Mark out the area the feature will be built in – this should be 1m (3ft) wide and at least 3m (10ft) long. You will also need an existing reservoir, or a new one can be built (see page 13). Clear the ground, removing any stones and rocks – pile these at the outlet end of the site. Now create a shallow pan-like shape for the stream. It doesn't need to be any deeper than 100mm (4in) in the centre and should have gently sloped sides. Its total width should be around 350mm (1¹⁄₆ft).

   To create the shape of your outlet, stack broken paving slabs or cheap bricks in a pile to create a height of about 400mm (1¹⁄₄ft). Then cover it with soil that you removed from the stream. Compact this and flatten the top of the pile to give room for the outlet stones.

2 Take the stones that you have for the stream and, with a hose and brush, give them a good scrub and leave them to

MATERIALS

Old paving slabs or cheap bricks

Hand picked, variously sized rocks

Fleece liner

Butyl liner

Soft sand

Cement

Pump and fittings

Hose and fittings

Conduit

Different-sized beach pebbles (10–50mm/¹⁄₂–2in) and cobbles (50–125mm/2–5in)

Small piece of timber

TOOLS

Groundwork tools

Building tools

Stiff hand brush

Bucket

1 Once you have cleared the ground, excavate a shallow, pan-like shape for the stream, giving it gentle slopes at either side.

2 Cut and fit the fleece liner into the stream shape and then do the same with the butyl liner, leaving extra liner at each side.

KNOW YOUR MATERIALS

The whole ethos behind creating a natural stream is to try and capture some of the exquisite beauty that is provided by nature. Each stream will be unique, it is the theory and construction that is provided here. However, if you really want inspiration then go and look at some real natural streams. Observe the journey or passage of the water and see how the rock and loose stone seem to guide the water's path – in reality it was the water that created their position. It is up to you how authentic and true you want your manmade version to be to the real thing. There is no right or wrong, just your own perception, so be creative.

dry. With the shape for the stream created, the liner that holds the water can be laid. First cut the fleece liner to the size of the stream's pan shape, leaving an extra 300mm (1ft) each side. Lay the fleece out across the stream and push it firmly into place. Cut out the liner in the same way, this time leaving a little more at either side than you did with the fleece. Drape the liner over the stream and work it gently into the shape, taking care not to stand on it.

3 Take the clean, dry stones and lay them around the outlet. First take the flattest stones and lay them in a stair-like formation up the middle of the pile, facing down the stream. These can be wedged into place using smaller stones, as can all the other rock work. Now choose the larger stones that will provide the sides to guide the water as it passes down the stream. Lay these around 150mm (6in) apart at the top, widening to around 250mm (10in) at the end of the outlet. With these in place, create the base layer of the stone mound that will conceal the outlet. The path of the water needs to be cemented to guarantee the water's route. Mix a 1:3 cement and soft sand mortar and point between the stones you have laid. Cover the stream and let the cement cure for 24 hours. During this time, the naturalized stones that mark the water's edge can be placed along the stream.

4 Attach the hose outlet before placing the pump into a bucket. Put the bucket into your existing reservoir and run the pipe up to the stream's outlet. The pipe itself should be disguised if at all possible. This could be achieved by concealing it underneath the rock, or perhaps by burying it inside a protective conduit pipe. The pipe needs to be positioned on top of the layer of stones that are laid on the mound. Protrude the pipe fractionally over the top of the first stone on the 'stairs' that you laid. Then check that the pipe cannot be seen from the front of the feature and that it will flow into the channel provided by the large side rocks. Lay a bed of mortar and press the pipe into place. Now lay the final layer of rocks on top and around the outlet to finish off the mound.

3 After you have laid the stones that will be the base layer for the stream, point between them and then leave to dry.

4 Once you have laid the pipe in place, lay a final layer of rocks on top of, and around, the outlet to finish it off.

5 You should create a natural flow for the stream by mortaring along the bottom of it with a strong sand and cement mix.

5 A natural flow needs to be created so mix up strong, soft sand and cement, a little wetter than last time, and shovel this out onto the liner in the shape of the stream. Begin at the top where the outlet stones stop. Start to smooth and spread the mortar into a bowl or pan shape down the stream. You should make sure that this mortar is laid about 20mm (³/₄in) deep. As you do this, be careful not to get any on the stones along the stream's edge as it would be difficult to remove.

6 When you are completely happy with the shape of the stream, take the smallest pebbles and cover the cement and sand mix that you have just laid. Make sure that you have given it a generous covering before tamping the pebbles down. Then take a small piece of timber and gently tamp the pebbles into the mortar. Avoid bringing the mortar through the pebbles to the top by overtamping. Also ensure that the pebbles creep up around the edges of the stream out into the surrounding garden.

7 The cobbles can now be arranged in and around the stream. The best way to try and avoid 'over kill' as you do this is to work up in size. First randomly lay some of the smallest cobbles around and then increase in size until the large beach cobbles are added. With all the cobbles in place you can then review the area and add or subtract any as necessary. As you do this remember that you are trying to create a natural stream. The bed of such a stream would be made up of small cobbles with some larger breaking the surface here and there. The edges should vary in size, leaving large stones prominent at the water's edge.

8 Now turn the power on at the pump. The water will flow out of the pipe outlet and among the stone with some pace. This will probably seem very fast to start with, but remember that even the quietest of streams move at some speed. Finally, adjust the stones and rocks along and in the water to improve the look and passage of the finished natural stream.

6 Once the mortar mix is in place, cover over it with the smallest pebbles and then tamp these into place with a small piece of timber.

7 Randomly place the pebbles into position, ensuring the smallest ones are done first and working up to the largest ones.

8 Once the water is flowing down the stream, adjust the stones and rocks to improve the water's passage.

waterfalls and cascades

planning for waterfalls and cascades

One of the most inspirational and dramatic conclusions to a stream or rill (see pages 50–53) is a waterfall. It can also be used mid-course to add extra interest. Such water management gives your garden high drama, sound and movement. If, however, you reduce the scale of a waterfall right down, and multiply the number of falls along the watercourse, you will have a series of gentle cascades that help move the water along its way.

Function and style Waterfalls and cascades provide an ideal way to introduce water into a terraced or sloping garden. In such positions the water in a stream or rill would gather too much momentum and cause the erosion of banks and water loss. In much the same way a stepped ramp works, the angle of a stream is reduced by using cascades. This gives you areas of tranquillity between the energy of the cascades and an overall balance is created.

Ponds and pools benefit enormously from the introduction of a waterfall. The power of falling water breathes life into the lower catchment pool, which is vital if you wish to introduce fish and encourage wildlife. It also clarifies the water, reducing algae and stagnation.

Our modern-day urban lifestyles may reward us in many ways but traffic and neighbourly noise can wear down the spirit. However the resonance of a mini waterfall or tumbling cascades, no matter how small, can revitalize a garden and mask unwanted sounds remarkably well.

Few gardens have the capacity for huge rock-built waterfalls. The sheer logistics of humping around giant rocks and boulders, coupled with the expense and construction skills needed, means that this style is rarely undertaken. More realistic answers are achievable, however. If you want a wall of water then you can use traditional materials such as natural layered York or sandstone. This would really suit a rural environment but, if you replace the natural stone with rendered blocks, reflective steel sheets or even marble and glass, the same style can be used to achieve the ultimate contemporary feature for a town garden.

Design choices A waterfall will be imposing within any garden design so you may want to use it as a focal point that can be seen from the house. The tantalizing

The dramatic effect of moving water.

A cascade made using containers.

Water trickles from a steel container.

A natural stone waterfall.

Waterfalls and cascades work particularly well in a tiered garden, where the various levels provide a natural fall for the water. Whether your feature is part of a magnificent modern ensemble of geometric shapes, dense planting and manmade materials (top left and right) or simply glides gracefully over the top of a more laid-back brick pool surrounded by simple planting, the movement of water will add another exciting dimension.

Waterfalls and cascades do not have to be huge – a simple trickle of water into a pool beneath works extremely well, especially when surrounded by planting.

movement of water will draw the eye and lead the viewer towards the action, inviting further inspection. People will want to stop and take a closer look, so it may be useful to provide seating. Cascades offer a completely different experience. They are usually placed along a watercourse so it is best to have a path beside the stream or rill to enable people to enjoy the feature up close.

On a smaller scale, a cascade can literally be made of three or four pans or bowls – the water just overflows from one into another. This gives you the opportunity to bring water close to your house and means that you don't have to rule out this type of feature if you have a small garden. Almost any style and combination of containers can be used, and planting arching grasses to act as a backdrop to the movement of water will enhance such an intimate design.

The catchment pool or reservoir for a waterfall or cascade should be in keeping with the overall style of the feature. It is often best to keep it low key, as it is not the primary focal point of the design. A sunken pool at ground level works well, but make sure that you have a pool large enough to take the impact of the falling water. Although there is inevitably some water loss it is surprising

> ### The tantalizing movement of water will draw the eye and lead the viewer towards the action...

how quickly a pool can empty. By simply adjusting the flow rate on the pump or placing angled stones under the fall to absorb some of the energy you should be able to control the water level.

Most people's senses seem to work overtime when confronted by a waterfall, as they are wonderfully tactile. In view of this, try to design pathways or standing areas that entice the onlooker to reach out and play with the curtain of water. Natural sunlight shimmers on the surface of a sheet of water so carefully position the angle of the fall to catch the best of the sun's rays. At night, by simply placing an underwater spotlight just beneath the water surface directly under the fall, you can illuminate the natural qualities of the moving water. This technique is perhaps suited to formal and modern styles of cascades where the repetition along a geometric rill can look astonishing from a distance when lit up.

Although you can plan meticulously, accidental changes often achieve the best results. This style of water feature truly provides some of the most exciting ways to play around with water. The following features incorporate some of these ideas and will inspire you to experiment with waterfalls and cascades in your own garden.

The natural effect of a large, rushing waterfall creates an exciting, dramatic effect when used in a large garden (top left). However, waterfalls and cascades can also be much more ordered and tame. For example, the geometric design shown above (top right) incorporates a series of pools and cascades to provide a formal yet calm focal point to the garden. This is surrounded by planting to soften the overall effect.

Water falls onto decorative shells.

A clinging wall of water.

Cascading metal waterfall.

Free-flowing water and steel.

contemporary WATERFALL

This feature is a wonderful use of space —
any garden with a wall, patio or border will
spring to life with this waterfall. The sound
and presence of the fall make it ideal for
the contemporary garden.

MATERIALS

Soft sand

High-density concrete blocks

Breeze blocks

Ballast and cement

Wall ties

Steel waterfall outlet

Fibre-reinforced render

Exterior plaster bead

Galvanized nails

Exterior masonry paint

Coping stones

Sharp sand

Bitumen paint

Hoses and fittings

Pump and fittings

Conduit

TOOLS

Groundwork tools

Building tools

Metalwork tools

Block saw or old panel saw

Angle grinder

Paintbrush

1 For this feature, you will need a clear, level area that is a
minimum of 2.5 × 2.5m (8¼ × 8¼ft). First, mark out the
shape of the foundation using sand lines – the back wall
is 1.8m (6ft) wide and the pool measures 900 × 1100mm
(3 × 3½ft). These are minimum dimensions – if you
want the wall to be higher, you will need to increase
the thickness of the blocks. Check the corners of the
excavations for square before digging using the 3, 4, 5
method (see page 14). Allow an extra 100mm (4in) width
all around the blockwork for your foundations. Dig out the
reservoir to the required depth and lay the concrete
foundation. This should be covered and left for 48 hours.

2 The rear wall can now be built using two courses of
concrete blocks below ground level and four courses
of lightweight blocks above. Concrete blocks are most
durable underground but the lighter ones allow the shape

*1 Once you have dug out the reservoir to the
required depth, lay the concrete foundation
in place.*

*2 Next, build the rear wall by using concrete
blocks below ground level and lightweight blocks
above these.*

KNOW YOUR MATERIALS

The fibre-reinforced render used on the wall has the ability to bond the structure and provide a resilient surface to an exposed wall. It guarantees the surface will not crack or deteriorate in any weather condition. The base of the pool has had a chamfer haunched around its edge – this is to strengthen the corners of the pool and guarantee the render gives a waterproof edge to the area that is under the most pressure. When the render is dry, before you seal it, go over it with a blowtorch and burn off the fibre tips that protrude from the smooth surface. Any fibre tip left will act as a wick and draw water from the pool to the block wall, emptying the pool quickly.

of the waterfall outlet to be cut out with greater ease. Use a 1:4 mortar mix below ground and a 1:6 mix above.

On top of the first course of concrete blocks, lay three wall ties to bond in the pool blockwork. Then lay four more courses of blockwork, leaving the middle block out of the last course because this needs a hole cutting out of it for the outlet. The pool construction can now be completed using a 1:4 mortar mix. With a hammer and chisel, cut a small section out of the top of a block on the last course – this will give you room to place your conduit pipes to take the pump hose and cable later.

3 Now, using the steel outlet as a template, draw the section to be removed – check that this section will be central to the pool when it is re-positioned back in the wall. Measure the width and length, allowing for an extra 10mm (½in) around both sides and the base for a mortar joint. When the top of the outlet is installed, it should finish flush with the top of the block. Using a block saw or old panel saw, cut down the two sidelines then

carefully chisel out the section. The block can now be built back into the wall and the final course laid on top and levelled. With a pointing trowel, clean off any excess mortar.

4 To fit the outlet, first make up a small amount of 1:6 mortar mix and spread an even 10mm (½in) layer over the bottom of the outlet void. Then place the steel outlet into the hole and use a small level to make sure that the outlet is tilting slightly towards the pool and is perfectly horizontal across its width. This is important as it will give you an even film of water. Now continue to point around the outlet, filling all the spaces and finishing the mortar smooth to the blockwork on the front and the back.

5 Once the main construction of the walls and pool has been finished, covered and left to dry out for a couple of days, the render coat can be applied. To ensure the rendering on the wall has protected, neat edges you will need to fix external plaster bead to them. Measure the

3 Measure the area that needs to be cut out for the outlet and then saw and chisel the block. Check the outlet sits flush.

4 Once the outlet is slotted into its final position, point all around it and smooth the mortar on the back and front.

5 You need to fix external plaster bead to the edges to ensure that the rendered wall will have neat edges.

edges of your wall and then, with tin snips, cut the lengths of beading. Fix them with galvanized nails, levelling the front and back top beads then fixing the side sections and upright. Pay special attention to how the corners meet.

6   Mix the 1:6 rendering mortar and add fibre-reinforcement, following the manufacturer's guidelines. Then, dampening the wall as you go, render the back wall as well as the pool's inside walls and base to an even thickness of 10mm (½in). This is done to give the corners of the pool extra strength. Build up a chamfer where the base meets the walls. Allow the render to dry for a minimum of 48 hours and then paint the main wall with exterior masonry paint.

7   Lay the coping stones around the pool, bedding them on a 1:3 cement and sharp sand mix (see page 12). They may need cutting down to size with an angle grinder. The joints can be pointed with a dryish 1:3 mortar mix. Make it similar to the stones in colour by making up some test samples and adding mortar dyes, letting them dry out until you have the right colour. Cover and allow the stones and pointing to dry thoroughly for 48 hours. Then apply two coats of bitumen paint to the inside of the pool and allow them to dry.

8   Measure the length of hose needed (from the pump, through the conduit then flat against the wall and onto the back of the waterfall outlet). Add another 300mm (1ft) tolerance and feed the resulting length through the conduit into the pool. Slide the hose over the copper pipe fixed to the back of the outlet and fasten using a jubilee clip. Screw clips to the wall that will secure the hose as it travels down the rear of the wall. Position the pump onto a block or a few bricks to stop sediment from the bottom of the pool getting into it. Attach the hose to the pump outlet with a jubilee clip and draw the power cable through the conduit to the power source. Fill the pool to the underside of the coping stones then turn the power on. Decide if the pump flow valve needs opening or closing to maintain the correct flow of water from the outlet.

6 Once you have mixed up the rendering mortar, you should dampen the back wall and add the render to it.

7 Lay the coping stones around the outside of the pool, bedding them down on a sharp sand and cement mix.

8 With the pump in place, you can connect the hose to the pump's outlet and secure it with a jubilee clip.

steel and
STONE WATERFALL

This piece of structural simplicity is the perfect partner for a stunning sculpture. The purity of the forms combine irresistibly with the gentle sound of water, creating a soothing, tranquil environment.

MATERIALS

Road pin or bamboo cane

Ten 150 × 50mm (6 × 2in) pressure treated timber posts

Prefabricated steel rill

Timber battening

Screws

Ballast and cement

Timber treatment

Copper sheeting

25mm (1in) copper pins

Flagstone

Bricks

Soft sand

15mm ($^2/_3$in) copper pipe

Compression fittings

Conduit

Hoses and fittings

90 litre (20 gallon) granite bowl

Pump and fittings

Rapid-hardening cement

Bitumen paint

TOOLS

Groundwork tools

Brushes

Building tools

Metalwork tools

Power tools

1   You will need an area 3m² (10ft²). Push a road pin or bamboo cane into the centre of the site. Place the end of your measuring tape over the cane and mark a circular shape at 500mm (1³/₄ft) along the tape using sand. This is the most important shape as it represents the basin. Now repeat this process to create semicircles at 800mm (2¹/₂ft) and 1.2m (4ft) along the tape to give the shape of the excavation. The footing needs to be dug out to a depth of 500mm (1³/₄ft) from ground level. Remember to keep the sides of the excavation upright and at the correct width.

2   With the footing dug out, the rill can be fitted. Take two pieces of timber that are about 1.5m (5ft) long. Lay them on top of each other, then measure 300mm (1ft) from one end and screw them together. This will give you the cradle support for the front of the rill. Ask for help to position the rill at the central point of the excavation then

1 Once you have measured and marked a sand circle at 500mm (1³/₄ft), mark semicircles at 800mm and 1.2m (2¹/₂ and 4ft).

2 Position the rill in the footing and support it with the cradle. Adjust the upright and level with a spirit level to give a small fall.

KNOW YOUR MATERIALS

The bowl in this feature is made from solid granite, which was handmade in China and imported. There was a ten week waiting period for the delivery of this basin. We felt this was worth the wait, but if you need to finish your project more quickly there are other alternatives. Half an oak barrel could be used or a glazed bowl to catch the water from the rill. You can use whatever you want as long as the capacity is similar to that of the bowl. You can also change the style dramatically by treating the upright timbers with clear preservative to naturalize the look. Alternatively, use mild steel instead of the copper sheet covering the rill post.

support the front of it with your cradle. Adjust the upright and level with a spirit level, ensuring that there is a very slight fall towards the basin.

3 The timber uprights can now be fitted at either side of the rill. Position these in the bottom of the footing to the side of the rill. Keep the heights of all the posts the same – check this with your level. Next, fix a length of timber between the two posts to give support. Now repeat this, erecting all the timbers on both sides of the rill leaving an equal distance between them. You may find that the posts will not create a complete semicircle – this is fine as the aim is a backdrop, you do not need to encase the bowl completely. Mix the concrete (see page 12) and pour it around the base of posts and rill. Leave it to cure for 48 hours. After 24 hours paint all the posts with timber treatment.

4 Due to the viewpoint of the feature, the upright post of the rill can be seen clearly through the space between the two posts. To hide this fix the copper sheeting into place. Measure between the two posts at the rear of the feature, the height from 50mm (2in) above ground level to the top of the posts and the rill. Mark all these measurements onto your copper sheet and cut the shape out with tin snips or a jigsaw with a metal blade. Then fix the copper to the back of the timber using 25mm (1in) copper pins spaced 100mm (4in) apart.

5 Within the circle for the basin excavate down 175mm (7in) from ground level and fill 100mm (4in) of this with concrete – this is the footing for the base of the bowl. Level it off and allow it to dry overnight. When the base is dry, mark around the flagstone onto the dry concrete base. Remove the slab and lay bricks on the inside of this line. Keep them level and ensure the good faces are pointing out. Cover the bricks and let them dry overnight. You will now need to measure the lengths of copper pipe needed for between the inside of the basin and the rear of the rill. Also measure between the base of

3 Fit the timber uprights either side of the rill and attach a length of timber in between them in order to provide extra support.

4 Hide the part of the rill that shows through the timber uprights by attaching copper sheeting using copper pins.

5 Take the flexible hose, which runs from the copper piping, and fix it to the rill outlet using a jubilee clip.

the copper sheet and 150mm (6in) short of the rill outlet as well as the upstand that leads into the basin. All these need to be measured with the 90° elbow compression joints taken into consideration and any pipe travelling across the open ground will need ducting in rigid plastic conduit. Cut and fix all the pipework, securing it with a bracket at the base of the rill. Attach a small section of flexible hose between the copper pipe at the bottom of the rill post and the tank connector at the back of the rill. Fix the hose into place with jubilee clips.

6 | Take the flagstone and drill a hole in the centre large enough for the copper pipe to pass through. Place the flagstone over the copper pipe and onto the brick edge – the flagstone is laid dry in case you need to access the pipework in the future. Check for level and then make any necessary adjustments.

7 | Place the bowl over the top of the pipe and onto the flagstone. It will be extremely heavy so ask for help when placing it in position. You can now fit the pump. Feed the power cable through a pre-drilled hole at the base of the bowl side and duct it out to the connection point. Next, place the pump onto a section of slab to keep it off the bowl floor as this will stop sediment from clogging up the pump. Fill the hole in the bottom of the bowl with rapid-hardening cement. Make sure you fill around all sides of the cable and pipe and finish level with the inside. Fill around the power cable with silicone and then apply two coats of bitumen paint around the pipe to seal the hole.

8 | You can now make final adjustments to the pump flow rate and check that all the joints are watertight. Dress the remainder of the site by laying paving, gravel or simply planting evergreen structural plants.

Alternative materials

This feature is very versatile. The upright timber could be replaced by existing trelliswork or the rill could start from within a banked area or a rock garden.

6 Drill a hole in the centre of the flagstone and place it over the copper pipe. Check for level and make any necessary adjustments.

7 Fill the void in the bottom of the bowl with rapid-hardening cement. As bitumen paint will be applied on top of it ensure that you give it a smooth finish.

8 With the water running, adjust the pump flow rate to suit the speed and rate the rill discharges into the granite bowl.

bamboo CASCADE

The passage of water through this clever bamboo cascade will intrigue and delight, while the gentle movement of water adds a zen-like calm to any environment.

1 | Decide on the position for your feature and work out where the reservoir will need to be. Put it on that spot and mark around it using sand. Allow 100mm (4in) extra all the way round for ease of fitting. Excavate the hole keeping the sides upright and the bottom level. Make sure that when the reservoir is in its final position its lip sits 50mm (2in) above ground level. When it is in place, fill around it with excavated soil and compact it in.

2 | Roughly lay out the bamboo feature on the ground to decide on the position for the bamboo outlet. Mark its location on the floor with a garden cane and then remove the feature.

Next, take the 600mm (2ft) long, 25mm (1in) wide galvanized pole and drive it into the ground over the top of the garden cane using a club hammer. Make sure that

MATERIALS

Reclaimed galvanized reservoir

Soft sand

Bamboo cascade

Oriental bamboo outlet

Garden cane

600mm (23½in) long, 25mm (1in) wide galvanized pole

Membrane

Butyl liner

Pump and fittings

Block

Hoses and fittings

Conduit

Angle iron

Chicken wire

Fuse wire or electrical ties

25–40mm (1–1½in) crushed slate

100–250mm (4–10in) slate paddle stones

Glazed bowl

TOOLS

Groundwork tools

Building tools

Angle grinder

Metalwork tools

I Once you have excavated the hole for the reservoir and put it in place, fill the surrounding area with soil, compacting it in.

2 Drive the galvanized pole into the ground with a club hammer. Keep 450mm (1½ft) of it above ground level.

KNOW YOUR MATERIALS

Bamboo: This is a very popular material for water features but it does need some work and preparation before it can be used. Within bamboo there are natural internal nodal membranes, which need to be removed because they would stop the flow of the water if left in place. They can in fact be taken out very easily by simply pushing a broom handle down the pole. You may also find it surprising that the fleshy inside and the hard exterior of bamboo is not actually waterproof. You therefore need to give the bamboo a generous coat of yacht varnish in order to ensure that you retain the water on its passage through or along the poles.

you keep the pole upright and also leave 450mm (1½ft) of the pole above ground level in order to support the bamboo pole outlet later on.

3 Cut and lay membrane on the ground under and around the feature. This will prevent weeds from growing underneath the crushed slate. Measure the amount of butyl liner needed to cover the area beneath the bamboo structure and then around the reservoir. Cut and fit this over the membrane. The hole can then be cut in the liner that will enable the water from the feature to return to the reservoir. (Use a craft knife to do this.)

4 Place the pump into the bottom of the reservoir on top of a block as this will prevent the pump picking up all the sediment from the floor of the reservoir. Lay the power cable into one of the corners of the reservoir and out onto the liner. Attach the flexible hose to the outlet inside the upright bamboo pole with a jubilee clip. The hose will travel down the pipe out at ground level to the reservoir.

Using a jubilee clip again, fasten the hose to the outlet on the pump. The power cable should then run through plastic conduit from the edge of the reservoir to the power source, where it needs to be connected by a qualified electrician.

5 Place the bamboo outlet over the top of the galvanized steel pole, making sure that it points towards the reservoir. Next, fit the angle iron supports over the top of the reservoir. These need to be cut using an angle grinder that has been fitted with a metal cutting blade. File down the ends of the angle iron to prevent puncturing the liner.

Once cut to size, lay the lengths of metal over the top of the reservoir and cushion the edges of the metal against the liner with membrane or extra liner. A small grill will be needed on top of the angle iron to prevent the slate falling through. This can be cut from chicken wire using tin snips and then be laid onto the grill. You may need to secure the two of them together – if so, use fuse wire or electrical ties.

3 Once you have laid the membrane and liner in place, cut a hole in the liner that will allow the water to return to the reservoir.

4 Fix the hose to the pump using a jubilee clip. This will ensure that water is taken to the outlet.

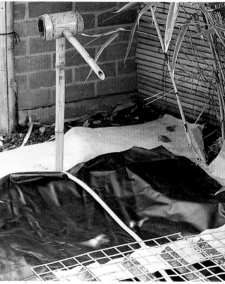

5 Once cut, lay the grill on top of the reservoir. Use membrane to cushion the liner against the hard edges.

6 | Now lay the crushed slate over the entire area and make sure that the liner is completely disguised. Lay the smaller crushed slate over the area first and build up to the large slate stones, which should be placed individually. Now position the cascade. It is important to have this safely on level ground so arrange the slate underneath to suit it, keeping the area as level as possible. (The feature has an integral gradient so you do not need to create a ground level fall.)

7 | Fill the reservoir up with water and, when it is full, turn on the power to the pump. The water will be flowing through the system at a particular speed so you can now adjust it to flow sensibly into the cascade and reservoir. The flow adjusting valve, within the pipework or on the pump, will give you this control. You may also need to make small adjustments to the outlet on the upright pole or to the angle of the cascade over the grill – try to carry out each of these changes while the water is still flowing.

8 | Ensure that you cover generously where the hose and conduit travel across the top of the liner with the slate. Position the bowl in front of the spout so that the water flows into the bowl before overflowing into the reservoir. Tilting the bowl towards the reservoir will help to do this. Make any final adjustments to the slate or feature to complete the cascade.

Alternative surroundings

The dressing of the bamboo cascade can be as simple or involved as you make it. Obviously the oriental theme is already in place, but the association with the Japanese garden always warrants some careful thought. You may not want to recreate a temple garden in your outdoor space, but with a few carefully chosen accessories you can still conjure up an Eastern atmosphere that will sit well with a contemporary or classic setting. It is worth bearing in mind that if you choose to sit the cascade on a patio, you will need to use different materials than if it were to be sited in a border.

6 Cover the entire area with slate, starting with smaller stones and working up to the largest. Try to keep the area as flat as possible.

7 Turn the water on and check the flow along the feature, adjusting the angle of the cascade over the grill if necessary.

8 Finally, position the bowl in front of the spout. You will probably need to tilt it towards the reservoir.

granite CASCADE

The light granite in this feature is striking against most backgrounds, while the tiered effect creates shadows and interest along with the dramatic movement of the cascading water. This cascade works well surrounded by water and marginal plants.

MATERIALS

Fleece

Butyl liner

Cement

Soft sand

Engineering bricks

38mm (1½in) plastic waste pipe
(2m/6½ft long)

Granite wheels (4 large, 3 small)

1 × 90° 38mm (1½in) bend

Silicone sealant

Pump, flexible hose and fittings

Bucket

Cobbles (various sizes)

Steel sheeting

8mm (⅓in) nuts and 100mm
(4in) long 8mm (⅓in) bolts

150mm (6in) length of wire

Fishing weight

TOOLS

Groundwork tools

Building tools

Metalwork tools

Pencil

Mastic gun

Felt tip pen

Power tools

1 Choose your site, which needs to be close to an existing body of water or reservoir. The area need be no bigger than 1 × 1m (3 × 3ft), but must be cleared of all debris and left with a smooth gradient towards the reservoir. Cut a piece of fleece to the size of the area you are building on and lay it into position. Then do the same for the butyl liner, but make it fractionally larger than the fleece. Be sure to drape the liner into the reservoir to ensure the water returns there after flowing down the cascade.

2 The cascade will be placed centrally on the liner. Mix up a small amount of 1:3 cement and soft sand mortar to lay the foundation bricks on. Lay a bed of mortar under each brick to form three sides of a square so the open end points away from the reservoir. The bricks should be laid level so use a spirit level to check this. It is extremely

1 Cut and lay both the fleece and liner, making sure that you drape the liner into the reservoir so the water will return there.

2 Lay the foundation bricks onto a 1:3 mortar mix and then ensure that they are level by placing a spirit level on top of them.

KNOW YOUR MATERIALS

The outlet cap is designed to disperse the water from the pipe evenly over the granite wheels' edges. The construction of the cap looks very difficult but is in fact straightforward. The fishing weight inside the tube acts as a restraint to the pressure of the water, so for a more powerful flow a larger weight would be used. There is nowhere for the water to go apart from the sides under the small gap provided by the cap, so this gives good control from a very simple design. The circle is steel, which will rust but won't harm the water or feature. The cap can be made from other sheet metals but if you decide to use stainless steel it is best to get it cut by a metal smith.

important to get this right as the whole feature's stability relies on the foundation bricks. Clean up the area once the bricks are laid and cover them to cure for 24 hours.

3 Construct the pipework for the cascade by using a 2m (6½ft) length of 38mm (1½ft) plastic waste pipe. There are seven granite wheels and seven mortar joints that are needed to secure them together, so calculate the total combined measurement of the granite and the joints, which will give you the measurement for the first cut. You need to take 10mm (½in) off of this measurement to recess the pipe at the top of the finished cascade. Cut the pipe with a hacksaw and connect one end of it to a 90° plastic waste bend. The other pipe needs to fit in the other end of the 90° degree bend and protrude the granite base stone by 75mm (3in).

Next, lay a 10mm (½in) layer of mortar on top of the foundation bricks. Place the pipework into position, making sure that the larger pipe that passes through the granite is roughly in the middle of the bricks. Now slide one of the larger granite wheels down over the pipe through the hole provided. With the wheel in place take a rubber mallet and level, and tap the wheel onto the mortar. Repeat this process until you are happy with the level of the base stone.

4 With the base stone in position you can complete the cascade by adding the other granite wheels. On top of the base stone you need to lay a 10mm (½in) mortar bed, but remember that the size of the next wheel is smaller. To prevent laying mortar where it is not wanted, place the smaller wheel on top of the base granite stone dry, and mark the width of the smaller granite wheel onto the base stone with a pencil. Remove the smaller wheel and apply the mortar inside the markings. Then slide it back on, repeating the method for securing it into place.

5 Repeat this process until you finish the stack with one of the large granite wheels at the top. Your last stone should be around 10mm (½in) above the pipe. There will be a gap around the pipe of around 3mm (⅛in), which will

3 Slide the first granite wheel down over the pipe, tapping it into the mortar using a rubber mallet. Then check it is level.

4 Once you have marked the area on the base stone that needs to be covered in mortar, put the mortar on followed by the next stone.

5 The final stone sits above the pipe. There is a gap around this pipe that should be filled with silicone sealant.

need sealing. Take a tube of silicone sealant in a mastic gun and carefully fill the void. Smooth the sealant round with a wet finger then cover and leave to dry for 24 hours.

6   The pump should now be positioned in the reservoir to provide the water for the cascade. Place the pump into a bucket, as this will cut down on the weed and debris from the existing body of water that is sucked up. The flexible pipe from the pump will need to be connected to the waste pipe that comes out from under the foundation bricks. The pipe should be hidden, so plan a route through planting or, as here, lie it flat against the liner so that it can be covered in stone later. With a jubilee clip, connect the end of the flexible pipe to the pipe at the bottom of the cascade. Tighten it well and lay the hose flat against the ground.

7   Next, cover both the waste and flexible pipes with small cobbles. Lay these out over the entire area of the liner. Build them up in size not only to cover the pipes but also to naturalize the area. Lay some in the water and the surrounding planting too to cover the butyl liner.

8   The outlet will now be dry so you can make the steel cap. Mark a 100mm (4in) diameter circle on a piece of steel sheeting with a felt tip pen. Lay this onto a thin sheet of plywood and, wearing goggles, cut the shape out using a jigsaw with a metal blade in it. Then mark the centre of the circle and drill an 8mm ($\frac{1}{3}$in) hole in the steel. Take a 100mm (4in) long 8mm ($\frac{1}{3}$in)-eyelet bolt and pass it through the hole in the steel. Screw an 8mm ($\frac{1}{3}$in) nut onto the end of the bolt – this will stop the bolt passing back through the drilled hole in the circular steel. The large fishing weight needs to be attached to a 150mm (6in) length of wire, the other end of which is fixed to the eyelet on the bolt. When you are happy that this is secure, lower the weight into the pipe and the steel circle will rest on top of the final wheel. Turn on the power to the pump and observe the water as it cascades over the edge of the granite from under the cap. Adjust the flow if necessary.

6 Tighten up the jubilee clip that connects the end of the flexible pipe to the pipe at the bottom of the cascade. Lie the pipe flat against the ground.

7 Cover over all the pipes with cobbles. Build them up in size in order to naturalize the whole area and also cover the liner.

8 Attach the large fishing weight to one end of the wire. The other end of the wire should then be fixed to the eyelet bolt.

fountains, springs & spouts

planning for fountains, springs & spouts

Fountains, springs and spouts collectively form the largest proportion of the water features that are available for gardens today. There is a huge diversity of features – from a simple overflowing urn through to the formality of a classical fountain. Inspiration can run riot with the technology of pumps and the diversity of modern-day materials so you can create exactly the type of feature that you want.

Function and style Fountains are extremely diverse in style and function, ranging from basic bubble features to huge dancing, multi-jet systems that have computer-controlled operations. Formal fountains are associated with high jets of water with varying spray patterns. They are ideal as centrepieces in small courtyards and, if you have the luxury of a long garden, make excellent focal points at the end of a vista. However, before you try to recreate Versailles in your back garden, there is a golden rule to follow when deciding the height of the jet – it should not exceed the radius of the basin or you will lose most of the water over the side. In windy sites you may have to reduce this further or use another style of feature.

You can be really creative with informal fountains as there is a huge choice – from contemporary stainless steel or glass to handmade folded concrete. Glass, copper and ceramic work very well with water and can be an amazing source of inspiration when creating a feature.

Nature has a simple way of filtering and cleansing ground water then delivering the source back to the surface through a natural spring. The bubbling brook created in a garden brings the same life and movement to your own piece of nature. If you place such a feature further away from the house then there is an ideal opportunity to create some mystery around it.

Wall-mounted spouts, on the other hand, can be placed in less than 0.5m² (1^3/$_4$ft²), which means that they are the perfect choice for smaller gardens. The great thing about such features is the sheer number of products that are available on the market – traditional animal and human masks are easily obtainable but you can use anything such as junk from a metal yard or a moulded plaster shell to create your own unique spout. The water will need to be

Bubble fountain among cobbles.

A stone spout.

Amorphous fountain.

Bamboo spout guiding water into a met

Fountains are extremely versatile water features. Formal or informal, the sound of moving water means they are very pleasing in both large and small gardens.

Do not be afraid to experiment with more unusual materials. The tiered fountain that is shown here (top left) is made up of metallic-finished plastic pillows.

If you have a small space, a bubble fountain can be a good feature (top right). Alternatively, use circular ceramic discs to create an elegant tiered fountain (above).

In a larger space, water can be jetted in many different directions using a system of spouts. Here the water is creating arches over a big pond.

collected in a reservoir of some kind. This could either be a pot overflowing into a hidden chamber containing the pump or a container placed in the ground that collects the water directly. There is so much choice of style that you will easily be able to find something suitable for your own particular garden.

Design choices   These features have perhaps the widest range of tricks and effects to design with so consider the following carefully before deciding on which type to have. Do you, for example, want to create a mysterious, intriguing feature that can't be seen straight away? By placing a fountain or spring behind a division along a pathway, the sound will draw people closer as it is hard to resist. Partially screening a feature with tall plants will make everyone want to peer into the feature too.

You don't have to have a lot of space to make a mysterious feature though. Surprise can also be created by using a grotesque wall mask that is covered in mosses with just a little trickle of water that enters a mossed-up stone trough. To create an aged appearance to the stone, simply paint on bio-yoghurt or liquid fertilizer. If you keep it moist then algae and lichens will start to appear.

Partially screening a feature with tall plants will make everyone want to peer into the feature...

Does your garden have a lot of surrounding noise, such as from traffic or other houses? If so, then you may want to use a fountain or spring to mask it. The trick here is not to overdominate your own space with noise or you could end up shouting at your family or guests in order to be heard. To avoid this, fill a bucket with water and trickle a hose into it from 500mm (1¾ft) to see how much noise it creates.

Moving water features can easily be combined with other features. For example, a natural spring could flow into a rock-filled pan that then overflows into a stone rill that takes the water on a journey to another part of the garden. It can then be collected in a chamber and be pumped back directly to the spring.

Moving water also gives you the chance to create some stunning effects at night so you should decide whether this is something you want to experiment with. A direct light placed high up and then shone on a fountain pool will throw a free light show onto a wall or temporary canvas. Alternatively, the ability of a single jet to hold onto light when it is lit from beneath using an underground source will never cease to amaze the viewer.

The projects constructed on the following pages provide you with all the inspiration and basic techniques that you need to create your own distinct moving water feature.

This evocative geyser (above left) will create an atmospheric feature in a larger garden. Alternatively you could use a sculptural spout (above right) to create a focal point within a pool. The water cascades down this centrepiece to provide an eyecatching element. These features have both been used to add interest to existing bodies of water.

A ceramic sphere with bubble fountain.

Sand-blasted, tubular glass fountains.

Oriental bamboo spout.

Domed fountain spray.

medusa head
WALL FOUNTAIN

There is nothing so enchanting as discovering a mysterious animated mask and fountain surrounded by lush planting in a secret part of the garden. This type of feature is ideally suited to smaller gardens where there is little floor area for a feature.

MATERIALS

Building sand

75 x 75mm (3 x 3in) post

Sleepers

Ballast and cement

Battens

Concrete slab

Reservoir tank 900 x 600m
(2³/₄ x 2ft)

Conduit

Coping stones

Oak timber plank (minimum
2.4m/8ft in height)

Galvanized carriage bolts

Wall mask

10mm (¹/₂in) soft copper pipe

15mm (²/₃in) copper pipe

Pump, hose and fittings

Brick or block

10–15mm (¹/₂–²/₃in) compression
elbow adapter

15mm (²/₃in) compression elbow

TOOLS

Groundwork tools

Drill

Woodwork tools

Building tools

1 Measure and locate the pool position and size with a sand line. Then mark out and position the post support and front sleeper. This should be placed approximately 1m (3ft) from the centre of the pool. Excavate the post and sleeper hole so that about a quarter of the height of the post will be below ground level, i.e. with 1.8m (6ft) above ground level there should be 600mm (2ft) below. Excavate an equal measurement around the post or sleeper (100mm/4in). Now position the post and sleeper into the hole and concrete to 100mm (4in) below ground level. It may help to use battens to hold the post as you do this.

2 Once the post concrete has gone off overnight mark out and excavate the reservoir, allowing space for a slab to be bedded on sand at the bottom of the hole (approximately 75mm/3in). This slab should be levelled both ways so that

1 Once you have excavated space for the post and sleeper and put them in place, concrete around them.

2 The reservoir lip should sit 75–100mm (3–4in) above the surrounding soil. Once this is levelled, position the ducting pipe.

KNOW YOUR MATERIALS

The mask: The head is made of Cornish granite and lead was used to create the serpents. These materials have the advantage of looking aged even though they are new. There are, however, many other traditional heads and masks available that are made of reconstituted stone or concrete. They do tend to look a bit harsh when new, so it helps to paint the surfaces with a bio-yoghurt to encourage premature ageing.

Oak upright: The weathered oak plank used here has been specifically chosen to add interest due to its contorted and twisted character. You can pick up all sorts of amazing one-offs by visiting your local reclamation yard.

the reservoir will also sit level. The height of the reservoir lip should finish 75–100mm (3–4in) above the surrounding soil height in order to allow for the base material under the coping stones, which should finish flush with the top of the reservoir. Once the reservoir is placed and levelled, the conduit for the pump hose and the electrics can be positioned. Drill holes as high up the reservoir as possible as this will dictate the final water level. Now the base material of concrete can be laid around the reservoir. A general concrete mix is suitable for the stones to be laid over (see page 12).

3 | After the concrete has cured overnight the coping stones can be laid. These should overhang the inside edge of the reservoir by 35–50mm (1½–2in) to conceal the top and the water line. Some of the coping stones might need cutting, so do this before laying them on the mortar. Once you are happy with the positioning of the stones they can be laid with a strong bricklaying mortar mix (see page 12). Finally the stones should be pointed with a dryish mix.

4 | Now the oak timber can be fixed to the post with galvanized carriage bolts. Try to fix one behind where the mask will be and another as low as possible so that the screws cannot be seen when the project is finished. Hold the fountain head in place and mark the position of the fixing and pipe holes on the timber. The hole through the post can then be drilled and the mask fixed into position.

5 | Having secured the mask, feed a 10mm (½in) soft copper pipe through the post, oak plank and mask so that it protrudes by 10mm (½in). The pipe can then be cut at a 45° angle with a hacksaw and pushed back into its final position. This angle needs to be cut for two reasons: firstly, the pipe slightly protrudes Medusa's head so cutting it will make it look less obtrusive. Secondly, the water will pour out of an angled cut on a pipe much better than it would from a flat-ended pipe.

Next, cut the end behind the post for connection to the upright 15mm (⅔in) copper pipe – this will be done later.

3 Once you have made any cuts and checked their positions, lay the coping stones onto mortar so that they overhang the reservoir.

4 Now fix the oak timber to the post using galvanized carriage bolts. Try to place the screws where the mask can cover them.

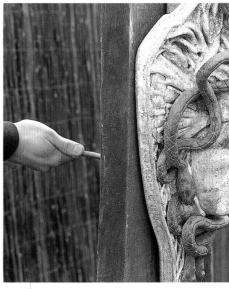

5 Once the mask is in place, feed a 10mm (½in) soft copper pipe through the post, oak and mask so that it protrudes out the back.

6   The pump can now be placed in the reservoir pool. Sit the pump on a brick or block to prevent any silt or grit entering the mechanics of the pump. Thread the hose and pump wire through the pre-drilled holes in the pool wall and into the ducting at the back of the post. Check that you lay the hose and cable as close to the pool wall as possible. Although the hose seems bulky and intrusive you will not see it against the black reservoir, which will be filled with water.

7   Fix a length of 15mm (⅔in) copper pipe to the back of the post. This connects the spout tube to the hose from the pump. You will need a 10–15mm (½–⅔in) compression elbow at the top of the pipe and a standard 15mm (⅔in) elbow at the base. You can now do the final connections at the base of the post. The hose is attached to the copper upright using a jubilee clip. A flexible hose is ideal, as it is easy to pass through the ducting and onto the copper pipe. The pump cable can be connected to an external junction or switch by a qualified electrician.

8   Fill the pool up to just under the pipe holes and then turn on the pump. Try to adjust the water jet so that it falls in the middle of the pool. You can do this with small adjustments to the pump flow valve.

Alternative materials

Although this mask is fixed to a weathered piece of oak plank, most gardens have a wall, garage or boundary of some description that can be used instead. These alternatives are just as effective – as long as you can get to the other side to do the pipework, they are ideal structures. If you are after a 'softer' approach, a post can be fixed within some hedging or taller planting (*Miscanthus* grass) to create a more subtle effect as it will suggest the head is actually peering out. Planting around the reservoir at the base of the feature so that the water disappears into a planted hole will further highlight the effect. Alternatively, you could use a narrower edging on the pool, dig in organic matter around the reservoir and then plant it up with ivy or vines to climb around the mask.

6 Make sure that you place the pump in the reservoir on a brick or block to prevent any silt or grit getting into its mechanics.

7 The connections at the bottom of the post can now be finished. Flexible hosing should be used and fixed to the pipe with a jubilee clip.

8 With the water running, adjust the speed and distance of the water by turning the flow adjusting valve on the pump.

glass cube FEATURE

This glass cube feature is ideal for a garden that has no room for a big water feature. It uses the bare minimum of space, but its impact and style competes with the most elaborate of waterfalls.

MATERIALS

75 × 75mm (3 × 3in) posts

75 × 18mm (3in × 1³/₄in) pressure treated timber

Ballast and cement

Zinc-plated screws

Wood preservative

Glass cubes

Vessel

Bolts

Rubber washers

15mm (²/₃in) and 10mm (¹/₂in) copper pipe and compression elbows

Porphyry flagstone slab

Sharp sand

Bricks

Pump and fittings

Hoses and fittings

Cavity-filling cement

Bitumen paint

Compression joints (conversion and size-reducing)

TOOLS

Groundwork tools

Building tools

Pencil

Power tools

Metalwork tools

Brushes

1 You will need a plot measuring 2 × 1m (6¹/₂ × 3ft) for the feature. Excavate two holes to a depth of 600mm (2ft) below ground level and 1.1m (3¹/₄ft) apart centre to centre, making the holes 300mm (1ft) square. Now centre the 75mm (3in) posts in the holes and check that they are exactly 1.2m (4ft) apart (outside to outside). To help you, use battens to support them. Use a 5m (15ft) tape to check that they are equal distance apart top and bottom. Now mix up your concrete (see page 12) and shovel it into both holes, tamping it down as you go. Ensure that the posts are upright again and support them with lengths of timber. Leave the concrete for 48 hours to cure.

2 Using a set square, mark your horizontal slats and cut them using a jigsaw or quality panel saw. Starting at 1.8m (6ft) above ground level, fix the first slat using zinc-plated screws and check for level. Then measure down 15mm

1 *Concrete your posts and check that they are still upright before supporting them with lengths of timber while they dry.*

2 *Once you have cut the timbers to the same length, fix them to the posts with screws, ensuring the spacing is consistent throughout.*

KNOW YOUR MATERIALS

When working with glass cubes it is best to keep them away from the building work until they are ready to be fitted to your surface so that they remain clean. When fixing each cube, it is important to use rubber washers in order to cushion the glass against the surface you are fixing it to. If the cubes are to be fixed to a brick or block wall, be sure to coat the wall with sealant, as this will prevent the excess water from the cubes and vessel causing the wall to corrode. Practically anything can be used as the reservoir (vessel) – this depends on your taste, garden and budget. Visit a reclamation yard or scrap metal merchant in order to see what is available.

(^{2}/₃in) and fix the second slat and repeat the process until you are 150mm (6in) above ground level, checking as you go that the slats are level. Then coat the trellis with wood preservative and allow it to dry for 12 hours.

3   To attach the glass cubes to the trelliswork you will need to know how high up the trellis your vessel sits – this will give you an approximate height for your bottom cube. Simply measure the height of your vessel and add the height of the base slab that it will sit on. Transfer the final measurement to the trellis from ground level. Mark a pencil line exactly in the centre of the panel. Your bottom cube should be positioned around 150–200mm (6–8in) above the top of the vessel. Using a pencil, extend the centre line up the entire panel (checking for upright using a level) – this will help when positioning the cubes. The top cube is placed three or four slats below the top of the panel and the middle cube should be an equal distance between the top and bottom. You should aim for a gap of 200–250mm (8–10in) between cubes.

Now mark and drill the bolt holes for each cube. Drill from the front to prevent unsightly splinters. Bolt the cubes onto the trellis using rubber washers in front of and behind the glass, which will prevent the bolts being in direct contact with the glass. Do not overtighten the bolts.

4   The slab that the vessel sits on has a void beneath it for pipework. It is created by laying four bricks on a 50mm (2in) sharp sand and cement (1:3) bed. The sides of the bricks should be flush with the edge of the slab so check the centralized position of the 450mm² (1½ft²) slab first. The tops of the bricks should be at ground level.

Using 15mm (^{2}/₃in) copper pipe and compression elbows, install the pipe that will travel down the back of the trellis. It should start 75mm (3in) below the spout and pass through the void. From there a 150mm (6in) upstand travels through the vessel's base to connect onto the pump.

5   The slab will need a 25mm (1in) hole drilled through its centre to allow the pipe and pump cable to pass through.

3 When you are bolting the cubes to the trelliswork use a rubber washer in-between the glass and bolt to protect the glass.

4 Once the bricks are in place, ready to create the void once the vessel sits on them, install the pipework that will connect to the pump.

5 Pull the pump's power cable through the bottom of the pot until the pump is positioned at the bottom of the vessel.

Lower the slab carefully over the pipe upstand and check its position and level. Also check that the hole in the vessel is 25mm (1in) in diameter then pull the pump power cable through it and the hole in the stone until the pump is positioned at the bottom of the vessel on a brick. Place the vessel over the top of the upstanding copper pipe and onto the flagstone. Fill the hole in the bottom of the vessel with cavity-filling cement until the cement is level with the inside of the pot. Paint the inside of the vessel around the pipework and power cable with two coats of a bitumen sealant and leave to dry for 24 hours. Connect the pump to the copper upstand using a short length of 18mm (³/₄in) flexible hose and jubilee clips.

6   At the top of the pipe that runs vertically up the rear of the trellis, fit the 15mm (²/₃in) side of the conversion compression joint. Measure the length of 10mm (¹/₂in) soft copper pipe that you need to run from this joint, through the point that is marked on the timber and down to 75mm (3in) above the first glass cube. Drill a hole at the point on the timber using a 10mm (¹/₂in) drill bit. At one end of the 10mm (¹/₂in) pipe cut an angle using a hacksaw in order to make it look more ornamental. Carefully bending the soft copper pipe, pass it through the hole until it is over the top of the first cube. Then fit the connecting end into the size-reducing compression joint. Adjust the spout so it is in the right position over the cube.

7   Fill the vessel up with water and turn the power onto the pump. The height of the water in the vessel is important to the success of the feature. This is because the water falling into the vessel is meant to be seen and heard. This is achieved by filling the vessel up fully, to within 50mm (2in) of the top.

8   Observe the flow of water through the cubes and then decide whether any adjustment is needed. If the fall of the water into the vessel is too erratic, turn the flow rate adjuster on the pump down. If there is hardly any water flowing through the cubes, turn the flow up.

6 *Once the copper pipe is bent and passed through the timber, fit it into the size-reducing compression joint.*

7 *Fill the vessel with clean water. You should see the level of water in the vessel at all times, so fill it up so it is 50mm (2in) from the top.*

8 *With the water running through the cubes, adjust the flow valve on the pump to change the overall speed of the water.*

volcanic SPRING

Springs and geysers give a feeling of natural energy, movement and power. This feature is a white water spring; the textured rock and smooth, elegant pillars of gushing water provide a dramatic sense of contrast.

1   As a guide you will need around 2m² (6½ft²). Mark out a 1m (3ft) diameter circle in the middle of the area using a peg driven into the ground and then attach a loose string around the peg. Measure along the string 500mm (1¾ft) from the peg, then mark the string at this point with a felt tip pen. Holding the string in one hand, travel around the peg in a circular motion, laying sand on the ground at the point of the mark. Continue until you have a complete circle marked on the ground, then remove the peg and start to excavate inside the sand line. When you are digging the hole, concentrate on keeping the insides of the hole vertical. The depth of the hole should be around 800mm (2½ft) as this feature has a large movement of water and so needs a reasonably sized reservoir.

2   The hole now needs to be screened with 50mm (2in) depth of soft sand. This is to protect the pool liner from

MATERIALS

Building sand

Pool liner

Pump, spouts and fittings

Bricks

Conduit

Steel rods

Membrane

Road mesh

Chicken wire

Grotto rock

TOOLS

Felt tip pen

Groundwork tools

Building tools

Metalwork tools

1 *Excavate the hole to a depth of about 800mm (2½ft). As you do this, ensure that you keep the sides as vertical as possible.*

2 *Start laying the liner from the bottom of the poo[l] carefully folding it as you go. It is best to do this wit[h] your shoes off, to prevent ripping.*

KNOW YOUR MATERIALS

Geysers: The key to an effective white water geyser is the nozzle fittings that are placed on the end of each pipe. A mechanism inside disrupts the flow, consequently adding air before you see the jet. Your choice will be influenced by how much noise and movement you wish the spring to create in your garden. When planning this feature think about the position. In order to give the best impression of excitement and surprise, you may choose to plant around the spring with grasses to give a 'lost world' look to the feature. But for a modern interpretation the volcanic spring could stand alone, within a seating area, to become an amazing conversation piece.

any objects in the soil that could tear or puncture it so you could use a fleece membrane instead. You will need to create a collection area surrounding the main reservoir to allow the splashes and excess water to drain back into the reservoir. Create this with soft sand too. This area needs to be roughly circular in shape, sloping down towards the reservoir. It should have a heaped lip to prevent water going further than intended. When you have compacted and spread out the sand you can lay the liner. Calculate the size of the liner required (see page 13) and, removing your footwear, start laying the liner from the bottom of the pool and work up, carefully folding and overlapping around the circular pool out onto the collection area. Leave the liner untrimmed until the reservoir is filled.

3   The pump work for this feature can be achieved in several ways – the submersible pump here has three heads that are attached via ready-made arms. There are individual flow adjustments on each of the heads, which gives you the flexibility to change the individual heights of each geyser. An alternative method of creating the same effect involves using three separate smaller pumps with a flow adjuster attached to each riser pipe. Remember that all pumps should sit on bricks within the reservoir to prevent debris from damaging the internal workings. Once the pump cable leaves the water feature, feed it through conduit until it reaches the junction box where it can be connected to the mains supply by a professional.

4   Cut four lengths of the reinforcing steel rod to completely bridge the reservoir and overlap by around 300mm (1ft) either side of the pool. Lay these equally across the pool surface – the rods may be sharp, so lay a fleece or membrane underneath to prevent damage to the liner. Measure the size of your reservoir pool and transfer this measurement to the sheet of mesh. Cut this size out and place it over the steel rods.

Cut a final layer of expanded metal mesh to size (you can use chicken wire) and lay it over the road mesh as before. All of the mesh work up until now has been large

3 The submersible pump used in this project has three heads that are attached with ready-made arms.

4 Once the road mesh is in place, put a layer of chicken wire over it. You will need to cut around the fountain heads.

5 Now that all the meshwork is completed, fill the pool up by using a hose and directing it through the mesh.

enough to arrange around the fountain heads, but the expanded metal grill needs holes cut into it first to allow the heads to come through. The weight of the stones will hold the mesh down so don't worry if it doesn't lie completely flat at first.

5 | After all the mesh work is in, the pool can be filled up. The quickest way is to use a hose. You need to fill it up to about 100mm (4in) from the top to provide an ample amount of water for this feature. Now turn on the pump to see how the springs work together. Take a few steps back and make a note of which springs need to be raised or lowered. Turn the pump off before making any changes.

6 | Now position your rock. In this case Grotto rock was used because of its character. The spouts that are sticking out through the grill need to be disguised. Begin to place the rock on top of the grill around the spouts. At first, position them directly next to the spouts, a little higher up so that the spouts are completely hidden. Then spread

the rest of the stone out to cover the entire grill, checking the overall appearance and making sure that no grill or liner shows through.

7 | Water will naturally evaporate from the pool and the hotter the weather the more water you'll lose. Therefore you should keep an eye on the water level every so often by removing one of the stones and having a look. If necessary, top it up with a watering can or a bucket until the level is 100mm (4in) from the top once again.

8 | With everything in place, and the water flowing, make the final adjustments to the positioning of the rocks.

Alternative materials

There are so many different stones and rocks for you to choose from that it is important that you go and see the wonderful selection. The best place to go is your local natural stone supplier; they will be more than happy to show you their wide range.

6 Start laying your rocks around the spouts and then work outwards to cover the entire grill, making sure nothing shows through.

7 Your reservoir will need topping up with clean water every so often. Bring the level up to around 100mm (4in) from the top.

8 Final adjustments to the formation and positioning of the rocks can now be carried out while the geysers are in full flow.

contemporary WATER BASIN

Unlike many features, this design provides the opportunity to place a stunning, modern water feature anywhere in the garden. As a patio feature, for example, this sculpture is a wonderful statement of art, design and expression.

1   The shuttering for the plinth of the basin is made first. Using 150 x 25mm (6 x 1in) planed timber make up a 700mm² (2¹/₃ft²) frame that is screwed together externally at each corner. Lay this on your proposed site and check it for square. Now mark out around the timber with some sand – keep the line about 50mm (2in) away from the edge of the frame. Remove the frame and dig out inside the sand marks to a depth of 100mm (4in). Then fill the hole to ground level with hardcore. Compact this with a hand rammer and check for level. Lift the frame into place and check the corners with the square. Take eight pegs (two for each side) and drive them down the side of the framework about 150mm (6in) in from each corner.

2   Check that the base is perfectly square before concreting. Also make sure that the pegs are below the height of the frame before the concrete is placed – this ensures you are

MATERIALS

150 x 25mm (6 x 1in) planed timber

Screws

Soft sand

Hardcore

Ballast and cement

Concrete sealant

Tile adhesive

Tiles

Grout

Basin, with pump, hose and their fittings already in place

Chicken wire

Membrane

Pebbles

75–100mm (3–4in) cobbles

TOOLS

Groundwork tools

Building tools

Brushes

Metalwork tools

Bucket

1 Once you have excavated the hole and filled it with hardcore, lay the frame back over and drive pegs around it to aid stability.

2 Fill inside the frame with concrete and level it off by dragging your spirit level across it, sliding left to right as you go.

KNOW YOUR MATERIALS

It is important to consider the way in which you surround the plinth of this feature with regard to maintenance and aesthetics. Here, the feature is surrounded with several different surfaces. Two sides of the feature have exposed aggregate patio along them, one has a planted border and the lawn cuts into the other. The bulky timber edging provides a strong edge to the entire area. The simplicity of the basin is in stunning contrast to the amazing tiled base. The same effect is achieved by using a simple surround of pebbles within the timber frame. Because this is positioned at the bottom of the tiles, the contrast is striking once again.

able to strike off the concrete easily. The volume of concrete needed can be worked out with a simple calculation (see page 12). A general concrete mix is adequate for this task, as it will be wet enough to work into the corners of the frame. Mix the concrete on a board near the base, then shovel it in making sure that any voids are filled, concentrating on the corners as you go. When you are happy there is enough in the frame, begin to level it. Take your spirit level and place it on the top of one of the sides of timber then, standing over the base, drag the level towards you sliding it left to right as you go. Remove the excess concrete and begin again – keep this process up until the concrete is level to the timber over the entire base. Be careful to replace any holes and remove bumps. A few gentle taps with a hammer on each side will encourage the water and cement to come to the surface, which will make tiling easier. Take care not to overtamp the concrete as this segregates the aggregate and weakens the slab. Leave this covered to cure for 48 hours before tiling.

3 | Your base should now be dry enough to remove the framework. You will need to unscrew the fixings and release the sides gently. Do not panic if there is the odd divot or hole – you can take care of this with tile adhesive. Give the base a quick brush over with a soft hand brush before sealing the concrete. The sealant needs to be painted over the whole base. Be generous as it hardens the concrete and stops the adhesive drying out too quickly, giving you time to position and fix the tiles. Cover and leave the base to dry for 24 hours.

4 | In a small bucket, mix your exterior tile adhesive to form a mix with the consistency of wallpaper paste. Now clean up around the base to prevent debris getting mixed up with the adhesive. Before you apply the adhesive to the top of the base, dry lay the tiles to check their position. Allow for an overhang around the edge, which will help the top and sides meet up neatly. When you are happy, remove the tiles and apply the tile adhesive. Using your float, spread the adhesive over the top of the plinth

3 Brush the base over and then seal the concrete by painting a sealant over it. Leave this to dry for 24 hours.

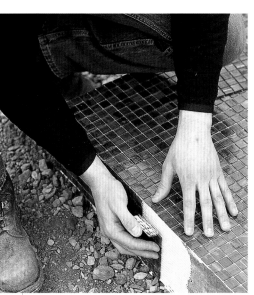

4 Apply your exterior adhesive and then lay the tiles on top of it, applying even pressure in order to ensure that they are bedded properly.

5 Once all the tiles are in place, spread grout over them using a rubber float to make sure that all the joints have been filled.

evenly. Then, with the toothed edge of the float, drag across the surface to create an even layer of adhesive. Lay the tiles on the top of the plinth, applying even pressure to bed them correctly. Check the overhang is even and remove any excess adhesive. Once the top has been tiled leave it for 24 hours, then tile the remaining four sides, paying special attention to the neatness of the top and side joint. Cover the base and allow 48 hours for it to dry.

5 Mix the grout up ready for spreading then apply an even layer of grout over the tiles starting on the top. Work it in with a rubber float and make sure that all the joints are filled, especially the edges. Remove the excess grout with the float and repeat the process on the sides, finally wiping over the whole plinth with a damp sponge. Cover the plinth up and allow it to dry for 24 hours before polishing the tiled surface with a clean dry cloth.

6 Now the basin can be placed onto the plinth. Ask for help as it is heavy. Place the basin onto the plinth keeping it

centralized. Take care not to disturb the tiles or chip the sculpture when positioning the basin.

7 Take a piece of chicken wire and cut a square section out that is large enough to cover the void for the pump. With tin snips, cut a small hole for the fountain hose to come through, then cover it with a membrane to stop debris collecting in the sump hole.

8 Wash a bucketful of pebbles in water and spread them around the fountain hose, covering the membrane but ensuring the spout is uncovered. Turn the power on to the pump and see if it needs any minor adjustments. You may need to move the pebbles around to suit the water movement.

Now dress around the tiled base with 75–100mm (3–4in) Scottish beach cobbles. These should be cleaned first before being placed. For the best results pile the cobbles several layers deep and arranged so that the base of the tiles are not visible.

6 Lift the basin onto the plinth. This is heavy work so ask for help. Take care not to disturb any of the tiles as you do this.

7 Take a piece of chicken wire and cut out a square piece to size, so that it will fit over the void for the pump.

8 Wash and place the pebbles over the wire mesh. Be sure to cover over the membrane while creating a natural pattern.

small water features

planning for small water features

When it comes to water feature design, powerful falls and complicated water channels can sometimes be over the top and unnecessary. Reducing the scale of your feature gives you flexibility over style, positioning and budget – enabling you to use innovative materials to create one-off designs. Inspirational finds in junkyards or garden shows will convince you that small features are often the most suitable for today's modern lifestyle and needs.

Function and style Small water features are perfect for those with smaller gardens who still want to enjoy having water nearby. For example, a tiny pebble fountain can easily be placed on a balcony or small patio. Or a little bird bath could be used to attract wildlife.

If you have children then a smaller design is by far the safest. This does not mean that you have to compromise on what you would want as smaller features can still visually stimulate and provide pleasure to all ages.

One of the best aspects of small water features is the fact that they are so easy to install and maintain. Indeed they can often be bought as ready-made kits that need few or no tools to be put together.

Design choices Large water features may be spectacular but because of their size can be limiting. Naturally, by reducing the proportions, a small feature has less impact on its surroundings. This actually provides you

with the opportunity to experiment with a wider range of exciting products such as innovative designs using ceramics, glass or reflective metal.

One of the beauties of a small feature is its ability to fill dead corners of the garden where a seat or pot would not quite work. This is a common design problem and can be confidently overcome by using a mini water feature.

One of the main things you must decide is whether or not you want to have movement within the feature. There is certainly plenty of choice if you do. Interconnecting containers come in a variety of shapes and sizes that allow water to trickle down from one into another. Alternatively, you may prefer to create one simple focal point by using a small water-filled pot on a plinth or a sphere that has water cascading down it.

A frostproof concrete bowl.

Moving water sphere.

Small designs can be humorous.

Water droplets clinging to reflective cylin

Small water features can be as simple or complicated as you want them to be. If you decide to incorporate movement within the design you may choose for the water to simply flow from one container or another (top left). Or you may prefer or more intricate design that results in a series of cascades (top right). A small, still feature, on the other hand, can welcome wildlife, especially if you use a natural, organic-looking design (above).

pebble CASCADE

This pebble cascade provides a well-designed and crafted vertical stack, which is so versatile it can suit any surroundings – from a contemporary patio setting to a lush border.

MATERIALS

Blue ceramic reservoir bowl (diam. 450mm/1½ft)

Beech cover comprising of:
1m (3ft) of 100 × 18mm (4 × ¾in) planed beech
450mm (1½ft) of 150 × 18mm (6 × ¾in) planed beech
1m (3ft) of 50 × 18mm (2 × ¾in) planed beech

15mm (²⁄₃in) copper pipe

15mm (²⁄₃in) copper water tank connector

Submersible pump with flow adjuster, cable and small hose

8 approx. 75–100mm (3–4in) glazed ceramic pebbles

10 rubber washers, diam. 18mm (¾in)

Feature can be ordered for assembly from suppliers (see page 127 for a list of suppliers)

TOOLS

Brushes

Sponges

1 | First, decide on your position for the pebble cascade as this will affect the route for the electrical supply. Lay out the ceramic reservoir bowl and the beech slatted cover with the copper pipe holding the ceramic pebbles. You should also have a mini-pump with a cable and a small hose – connect that to the copper pipe at the base of the cover. It can be secured with a jubilee clip if necessary.

2 | Make sure the reservoir bowl is stable and on firm ground. Check that the ground is level. Fill the bowl with clean water and carefully place the cover over the reservoir. Check that the cable is not trapped under the hood. Next, place the remaining ceramic pebbles on top of the existing pebbles. It is important to place the supplied rubber washers between each stone to stop water running inside the stack and losing the effect.

1 Connect the small hose to the copper pipe that will hold the pebbles at the base of the cover.

2 Once the cover is secured stack the pebbles, remembering to insert a rubber washer between each one.

KNOW YOUR MATERIALS

Pebbles: These beautifully crafted ceramic pebbles look delicate when they are subtly balanced on top of each other. Although they look precarious, the copper pipe that carries the water through the centre gives the stack great stability.

Timber: The timber-slatted base is made from planed beech, which has been varnished. In order to prevent excessive water loss the timber beading strips have been fixed to the top of the base. There are also additional timber beads placed on the underside to help position the stack over the bowl.

spherical FOUNTAIN

This project allows you to use a small body of water in a creative and effective way. Its reflective glaze and subtle sound make it perfect for any seating area.

MATERIALS

UPVC reservoir

Submersible mini-pump

Glazed spherical fountain, 400mm (1¼ft) diam. with an 18mm (¾in) hole in the top

450mm (1½ft) hose

2 × 40kg (88lb) bags of mixed beach pebbles (30–100mm/1¼–4in)

Feature can be ordered for assembly from suppliers (see page 127 for a list of suppliers)

TOOLS

Groundwork tools

Building tools

Watering can

Bucket

Sponge

1 Firstly, you need to decide on the position of the fountain. Physically move the sphere around the garden to find the best site. As you do this, ensure an easy route can be achieved for the supply of power to the feature.

Clear around the area and dig out the hole in which the 'top hat' reservoir will sit. Be sure to keep the reservoir clean and free from soil, as the water for the fountain will be stored in it. Fit the reservoir firmly into place and check across the top for a good level surface using a spirit level, because you will be placing the sphere onto it later.

2 Now with your watering can, fill the reservoir up with clean water and place the mini-pump into the centre of the plastic bowl. Feed the hose from the bottom of the sphere through the hole provided in the lid of the reservoir. Position them both next to the reservoir and attach the hose to the outlet on top of the mini-pump.

1 Once you have decided where you want the feature, clear a space for the reservoir and then position it.

2 Next, connect the adjustable pump to the hose that comes from the top of the spherical fountain. Secure it with a jubilee clip.

The vibrantly glazed spherical fountain works because of its simplicity. The top of the fountain is a concave pool that fills with water and overflows, rippling down the side of the vessel. Extra emphasis is added by the ripple-effect glaze.

The reservoir is made of durable UPVC and is ideally suited to small light features that need a minimum volume of water to operate.

The inside of the pool is a good opportunity for you to be creative. There is a wide range of materials that could be used – crushed glass, stainless steel shards, white marble pebbles or rusty washers would all give a different and very effective finish.

To cover the plastic reservoir use a range of 40–100mm (1¹/₄–4in) beach pebbles. These will look stunning when wet.

3 | With the hose attached to the pump, carefully place the lid with the sphere into their correct positions on top of the reservoir. Test the flow by turning on the pump. The basin in the top of the sphere will permanently be filled with water and the pump will create the fountain, which in turn will cause the water to overflow down the glazed sides of the sphere. The water should fall over the edge of the sphere equally all the way around because you levelled the surface in step one.

Take a bucket and sponge and clean the pebbles before laying them around the base of the sphere. It is important to do this as any dirt or grime on the stones will be washed off into the reservoir and then re-circulated over the feature, causing unnecessary cleaning. Position the pebbles to disguise the top hat reservoir and complete the overall look of the feature. Check that all cables are covered with pebbles too.

ceramic POOL

The success of this little ceramic pool is its very simplicity. The gentle curve of soft water provides just a suggestion of movement, while a scattering of marble pebbles in the base of the bowl gives the feature a look of natural spontaneity.

1 Find the right position for your feature in the garden by moving it around and taking note of the best place. It is often a good idea to put it in very different settings and leave it in each one for a while before deciding whether or not you can get the full benefit of the feature from that location. Be imaginative with your placing of it as this particular type of feature can live almost anywhere. When it has a spot in the garden, create a clear space in which the bowl can be positioned and levelled. Be sure that the power to the pump will have a reasonably easy route. It is best if the cables are hidden as the appearance of the pool will be tarnished if the source of its energy is exposed.

2 Take the mini-pump and position it in the centre of the pool. The point at which the cable leaves the side of the pump needs to be opposite the small hole for the cable

MATERIALS

400mm (18in) diam. glazed ceramic reservoir

A mini-pump with flow adjuster

125mm (5in) diam. ceramic dome with an 18mm (³/₄in) central hole in the top

5kg (11lb) of 18–25mm ³/₄–1in white marble pebbles

Feature can be ordered for assembly from supplier (see page 127 for a list of suppliers)

TOOLS

Watering can

Bucket

Sponge

Soft hand brush

1 Clear around your chosen area, position your reservoir and then check for level using a small boat level.

2 Place the mini-pump in the centre of the bowl and feed the cable through the side of the reservoir bowl.

The ceramic pool is one of the simplest ways to introduce water to any patio border or even the smallest of balconies.

The particular glaze finish that was used here contains hues of greens and blues with some subtle rusty markings. This enables it to be positioned almost anywhere in the garden, whether on a timber deck or nestled among planting.

The power cable needs to be considered. This is extremely important if you are positioning the feature in a border. If the cable needs to travel a distance, or is buried, a protective conduit or tubing should be used. Employ a qualified electrician to install your pump for you.

Once the pump is centrally positioned place the pump cover over the pump. Turn the pump on and make any final adjustments.

in the top of the pool's rim. Leave the cable without a plug for now and feed it through the hole in the rim of the pool. Continue to feed it along until it lies neatly in the bottom of the pool. Then fill the pool up with clean water from your watering can until the pump is covered.

3 Take the ceramic dome provided and place it over the top of the pump. Ensure that the cable passes under the section cut out of the dome's base to ensure a neat finish. The outlet from the pump for the bubble fountain should be lined up directly beneath the hole provided in the top of the dome. Turn on the power and check that the fountain is passing through the hole in the dome with ease. If all is well, top up the water in the pool to just beneath the hole in the rim. Wash and place small white marble pebbles inside the pool, evenly spaced for best effect. Then dress around the bottom of the feature.

tiered CASCADE

An exciting movement of water, through tiered, changing levels, provides interest and sound from vessel to vessel. The design and journey of this wonderfully crafted cascade can easily be arranged to suit the individual garden.

1 | Decide where your feature is to be positioned and then put the base bowl in place. The largest bowl, which acts as a reservoir, needs to be at the lowest point so that the others can be arranged at sufficient heights for the feature to work. Feed the cable for the mini-pump through the hole provided in the rim of the base bowl. You also need to feed the hose that will carry water from the pump to the jug through this hole. Next, the glazed dome needs to be placed in the base bowl over the pump to disguise and protect it.

2 | Now arrange the stands and other bowls, ensuring that the water will flow smoothly from one to the next without spilling or cramping the feature together. The distance of the stand and jug (which is the source) from the base bowl will be determined by the size of the bowls provided with the feature.

MATERIALS

Ceramic reservoir bowl

Mini-pump and hoses

125mm (5in) diam. ceramic, dome-shaped pump cover

225mm (9in) diam. ceramic stand

150mm (6in) diam. ceramic stand

300mm (1ft) ceramic pan with lip

250mm (10in) ceramic pan with lip

Ceramic jug with inlet hole for hose

Such features can be ordered for assembly from suppliers (see page 127 for a list of suppliers)

TOOLS

None needed

1 Once you have positioned the base bowl and fed the hose through the hole provided, cover the pump with the dome.

2 Now arrange the other bowls and stands, making sure that the water flows smoothly and everything is stable.

This particular cascade is made of frostproof ceramic, which is a necessity in colder climates. However, not all ceramic material is frostproof so make sure that you check with the supplier before you buy. If there is any doubt, empty the feature and dry out the pump during spells of sub-zero weather in order to avoid damage from expanding ice.

One of the problems with this type of feature is the lack of stability due to the number of components. If you have uneven ground, lay one or two slabs just under ground level to give a stable base for your feature. The slabs can then be covered with decorative bark or gravel.

Fill the reservoir bowl with clean tap water up the brim and then turn the power on and adjust the direction of the flow.

3 Finally, fill the large bowl with clean water until the pump is covered. Turn on the power to the pump and observe the water's passage. Move and adjust the flow where necessary in order to give the best movement of water. When you are happy with the feature, dress around the base of the stands and bottom bowl to complete the setting for this cascade.

Alternative positioning

The positioning of this feature will really depend on the look that is to be achieved. A country setting would naturally lend itself to this particular feature, mainly because of the material and the fact that a jug is incorporated. However, there is room for this design of feature in a modern and contemporary setting too. You could change the arrangement to a formal line of equally spaced bowls, perhaps contrasted against a dark slate patio.

index

suppliers

The publisher and photographer would like to thank the following for permission to take photographs of their gardens and water features:

Susan and Alastair Alexander: p125 (designer: Mark Braniff)

Sue and Alastair Brown: p63 (designer: Kate Dix at Plum Garden Designs)

Mr and Mrs Chambers, Kiftsgate Court, Gloucestershire (National Garden Scheme): pp6–7; p28 far left; p29 below (designer: Simon Allison)

Ian Clien: p121

Fairhaven Garden Trust, Norfolk (open to the public): p51 below

Monique and David Gregson, 2Fish Gallery, Diss, Norfolk: p19; p52; p74

Ian Griffiths: p33

The Hannah Peschar Sculpture Garden: p28 far right (landscape designer: Antony Paul); p29 above left (landscape designer: Antony Paul); p31 below far left (landscape designer: Antony Paul); p51 above right (landscape designer: Antony Paul); p72 far left (landscape designer: Antony Paul); p75 above left (landscape designer: Antony Paul); p96 (Swaylines, designer: Andrew Ewing); p97 above right (Water Sculpture, designer: Ben Barnell); p97 below centre left (designer: Tzubai); p117 below (Pebble, designer: Jean Lowe)

Catherine Heatherington (designer): p77

Catherine Horwood (NGS): p119

Chris Knows: p116 far left

Elizabeth Mactyrue-Brown, Hertfordshire: p73 below (designer: Richard Key)

Johann and Gail Meeke: p111

Mickfield Water Garden Centre, Mickfield, near Stowmarket, Suffolk (for allowing us to take various photographs of water plants, fish and other products)

Rousham, Oxfordshire (open to the public): p50 far right

RHS Chelsea Flower Show 2001: p28 centre left, p31 above left and p53 above left (A Real Japanese Garden, The Daily Telegraph); p28 centre right; p29 above right (Laurent-Perrier/Harpers & Queen, designer: Tom Stuart-Smith); p30, p51 above left and p95 above right (London Borough of Barnet Skills Training Centre, designer: Frank Gardner); p31 above right (Blue Circle Garden, designers: Carole Vincent and Jill Mellor); p31 below centre

left (Brinsbury College); p31 below centre right and below far right; p50 far left (designer: Brian Alabaster); p53 below far right; p72 centre left; p73 above right and p75 below centre left (The Curc Garden, designer: Andy Sturgeon); p75 above right (City Space, designer: Mark Antony Walker); p75 below centre right and below far right (designer: Simon Percival); p94 far left, centre left and far right; p94 centre right and p117 above left (designers: Stoltzman and Thomas); p95 above left; p97 above left; p116 far right

RHS Hampton Court Flower Show 2001: p8; p9 below left; p9 below right (Cherry Burton Garden Design); p10 below left and above right; p11 (The Tree of Knowledge, Richmond Adult Community College); p18; pp26–7 (Eastern Promise, Dorset Water Lily Company); p45 (A Swimming Pool, Anglo Aquarium Plant Company, designer: David Lloyd-Morgan); pp48–9 and p75 below far left (P&O Cruises Tropical Experience, designer: Jane Mooney); p50 centre left (Vivid Space Design); p50 centre right (The Paradise Garden, designer: Elizabeth Apedaile); p53 above right, below far left, below centre left and below centre right; pp70–1 (An English Garden Designer in France, designer: P Dyer); p72 centre right and far right; p73 above left (Urban Chic, Mitsubishi); pp92–3, p97 below centre right and p117 above right (2001 A Garden Odyssey, Farrscape Design); p95 below; p97 below far left and below far right; pp114–15 (The Princess and the Frog, Shani Lawrence Garden Designs); p116 centre left and centre right

Shaun and Pauline Stringer: p55, p123

Writtle College: p20 below left; p21 below left and above right; p37; p44; p59; p67; p81; p85; p89; p99–8; p103; p107

Yarnton Nurseries, Oxon: p20 above right

The publisher and stylist would like to thank the following for their kind assistance in supplying materials and decorative items:

The authors recommend the use of OASE pumps, filters and liners when building any garden water feature. For information on the availability of OASE products contact: OASE (UK) Ltd 01264 333 225 www.oase-pumpen.com

Brian Duffy, 01978 265 315, duffyglass@hotmail.com: glass cube p102

CED Ltd, 01708 867 237, sales@ced.ltd.uk: York stone copings p32; porphyry paving p36; slate chippings and marble cobbles p40; various sandstone rocks and beach pebbles p66; slate paddle stones p84; slate coping stones p98; grotto rock p106

Clifton Nurseries, 5A Clifton Villas, Little Venice, London W9 2PH, 020 7289 6851, e-mail@clifton.co.uk, www.clifton.co.uk: ferns, ivy, bamboo and topiary p67, p81, p99

Elephant, 020 7637 7930

cvo Firevault, 020 7255 2234, www.cvofirevault.co.uk

Gardens & Beyond, 47 Highgate High Street, London n6 5JX, tel 020 8340 3409, fax 020 8340 3410, design@gardensbeyond.com, www.gardensbeyond.com: wooden loungers pp55, 63 and 121

Granite Connection, 01773 533 090, sales@graniteconnection.co.uk: granite bowl (granite connection) p80; granite wheels (granite connection) p88

Green Door, 020 7686 0701, helendewolfe@aol.com: contemporary basin p110.

Habitat, 0845 601 0740, www.habitat.net: glass jug and glasses on table p111

The Holding Company, 020 7352 1600, www.theholdingcompany.co.uk

Ironage Developments Ltd, 01462 485 395, ironage@freeuk.com: wet and dry pool p36; copper sheeting p54; steel sides p58; stainless steel p62; steel chute p76; steel rill p80

Jungle Giants, 01584 819885, bym@junglegiants.co.uk: bamboo cascade p84

The Lacquer Chest, 75 Kensington Church Street, London W8 4BG, 020 7937 1306: metal table and chair p99

Lassco, 020 7739 0448, www.lassco.co.uk: Medusa fountain head p98

Lloyd Christie, 103 Lancaster Road, Notting Hill, London W11 1QN, tel 020 7243 6466, fax 020 7313 6582, info@lloydchristie.com, www.lloydchristie.com: metal lounger p37

The Old Bake House, 01243 573 263: pebble cascade p118; spherical fountain p120; ceramic pool p122

The Pier, 020 7637 7001, mail order 020 7814 5004, www.pier.co.uk: lantern p55; urn p99

Rawlinson Garden Products Ltd, 01270 506 900, www.rowgar.co.uk: softwood sleepers p56

S.B Evans & Son, 020 7729 6635, evans@thecitygardenpottery.co.uk: tiered cascade p124

Tropical Surrounds, 01264 773 006: bamboo, willow and heather screening

author's acknowledgments

Our thanks go to our editor, Natasha Martyn-Johns, for her humour and patience and to Juliette Wade for her fantastic photography during long summer days. A special thank you to Claire Musters for keeping us focussed throughout. We would also like to thank all of the generous people who kindly let us use their wonderful gardens for the book.

We must also say a huge thank you to all our friends at Writtle College, particularly Greg Allen and all the ground staff and technicians who were so generous with their time and resources. Thanks also to Mark Winters and Chris Wright at OASE for their expertise and technical know-how. Their foresight and generosity in backing this project has made our lives a lot easier.

Finally we would like to thank David Campbell, Jon Roffe and Chad Sheldon for their constant help throughout the project, and a heartfelt thank you must go to Mark's wife Emma for everything she has done, and continues to do, in support of our dreams and ambitions.

The authors run their own design and construction company, Musa Designs, and can be contacted at info@musagardens.fsnet.co.uk

First published in 2002 by Murdoch Books UK Ltd

Copyright© 2002 Murdoch Books UK Ltd

ISBN 1 85391 973 X

A catalogue record for this book is available from the British Library.

Commissioning Editor: **Natasha Martyn-Johns**

Editor: **Claire Musters**

Managing Editor: **Anna Osborn**

Design Manager: **Helen Taylor**

Photo Librarian: **Bobbie Leah**

Photographer: **Juliette Wade**

CEO: **Robert Oerton**

Publisher: **Catie Ziller**

Production Manager: **Lucy Byrne**

International Sales Director: **Kevin Lagden**

Colour separation by Colourscan, Singapore

Printed by Tien Wah Press in Singapore

Murdoch Books UK Ltd
Ferry House, 51–57 Lacy Road
Putney London, SW15 1PR, UK
Tel: +44 (0)20 8355 1480
Fax: +44 (0)20 8355 1499
Murdoch Books UK Ltd is a subsidiary
of Murdoch Magazines Pty Ltd.

Murdoch Books®
GPO Box 1203
Sydney, NSW 1045, Australia
Tel: +61 (0)2 8220 2000
Fax: +61 (0)2 8220 2020
Murdoch Books® is a trademark of
Murdoch Magazines Pty Ltd.

UK Distribution
Macmillan Distribution Ltd
Houndsmills, Brunell Road
Basingstoke, Hampshire, RG1 6XS, UK
Tel: +44 (0) 1256 302 707
Fax: +44 (0) 1256 351 437
http://www.macmillan-mdl.co.uk